The Freelancer's Budget

Managing Irregular Income, Planning for Taxes, and Stopping the Invoice-to-Invoice Cycle

Ryan Papadopoulos

DISCLAIMER

This provides general financial information and strategies for freelancers managing irregular income. It is not intended as financial, tax, legal, or professional advice. Every person's financial situation is unique, and the strategies discussed may not be appropriate for everyone.

The examples, calculations, and scenarios presented are for illustrative purposes only and should not be considered personal recommendations. Tax laws, regulations, and financial products change frequently, and information that is accurate at the time of writing may become outdated.

Readers should consult with qualified financial advisors, tax professionals, and legal counsel before making significant financial decisions or changes to their business structure. The author and publisher disclaim any liability for financial decisions made based on information in this book.

While every effort has been made to ensure accuracy, no guarantees are made regarding the completeness or reliability of the information provided. Use of this information is at your own risk.

ACKNOWLEDGMENT

This exists because of the countless freelancers who've shared their struggles, successes, and hard-won financial wisdom over the years. Your stories of navigating irregular income, building stability from chaos, and learning through trial and error informed every page.

To the financial advisors, accountants, and bookkeepers who work with self-employed people daily, thank you for your patience in explaining tax strategies, retirement options, and money management systems that actually work for variable income.

To everyone who's ever felt the stress of wondering if next month's invoices will arrive in time to cover this month's rent, who's scrambled to save for quarterly taxes they forgot about, or who's realized too late that their emergency fund was actually just next month's operating capital, this is for us.

May we all build systems that let us sleep at night.

The Freelancer's Money Problem

Most freelancers spend their first few years thinking the problem is making enough money, when actually the problem is that money shows up whenever clients feel like paying and disappears just as fast, leaving us wondering where thousands of dollars went even during months when we earned well above what we thought we needed to survive. We know we made good money last month because we remember invoicing those clients and seeing decent numbers hit the bank account, but somehow rent is due and we're checking the balance three times hoping the number changed, which it never does, and this happens so often we start thinking maybe we're just bad with money even though we're smart enough to run entire businesses by ourselves.

The truth nobody told us before we went freelance is that earning $5,000 one month and $2,000 the next creates completely different problems than earning $3,500 twice, and traditional budgeting advice built for people with steady paychecks becomes actively harmful when we try following it because we end up either starving ourselves during good months or overspending during bad ones, neither of which actually works. Those personal finance books sitting on our shelves keep telling us to make a monthly budget based on our income, track our spending against it, and adjust as needed, which sounds great until we realize our income next month could be anything from zero to ten thousand depending on which invoices get paid and whether that new client actually signs the contract, making the whole "budget based on income" thing completely impossible.

We're not bad with money. We're using systems designed for a different reality, and then beating ourselves up when those systems fail, which they always do because they were never meant to handle the kind of income variability that comes with freelancing. The freelancer who makes $60,000 a year faces entirely different challenges than the employee making $60,000 a year, even though on paper those numbers look identical, because one person knows exactly what's hitting their account on the first and fifteenth of every month while the other is tracking twelve different invoices that might get paid tomorrow or might sit in someone's email for another six weeks.

Breaking free from the invoice-to-invoice cycle where we're always waiting for the next payment to cover this month's expenses requires building completely different systems than what works for regular employment, and those systems start with accepting that our income will always vary and planning around that reality instead of pretending it won't. We can't eliminate the variability, clients will always pay on their own schedule and project work will always be unpredictable, but we can build a financial structure that turns that chaotic income into stable cash flow that lets us sleep at night without checking our bank balance at 2am.

The real transformation happens when we stop trying to budget our actual variable income and instead create a predictable salary we pay ourselves from that variable income, which sounds impossible until we understand how the buffer system works and why separating our business money from our personal money changes everything about how we experience financial stress. Once we've got that separation in place and we're paying ourselves the same amount every month regardless of what clients did or didn't pay, budgeting becomes simple again because we're working with a known number instead of a guess, and that known number stays consistent even when business income swings wildly.

Most freelancers who feel broke despite earning decent money are actually experiencing a cash flow timing problem, not an income problem, and fixing the timing issue often matters more than increasing total earnings because an extra thousand dollars a month doesn't help if it shows up three months late and we've already maxed out the credit card covering the gap. Getting ahead of our expenses by just one month, where we're using last month's income to pay this month's bills, eliminates probably eighty percent of the financial stress we deal with even if our total income stays exactly the same, which it usually doesn't because once we're not constantly scrambling we can actually be selective about which clients we work with and which projects we take on.

The other massive piece nobody warned us about is taxes, specifically the part where we owe both halves of Social Security and Medicare because we're both the employer and the employee, which comes out to 15.3% right off the top before we even get to regular income tax. Regular employees never see that employer half because it gets paid behind the scenes, so when we went freelance and suddenly had to cover the whole thing ourselves, many of us got blindsided by tax bills that wiped out months of savings or forced us into payment plans with the IRS that charged penalties and interest on top of what we already owed.

Setting aside 25 to 30% of every single payment for taxes sounds extreme until we do the math and realize that's actually about right when we factor in self-employment tax plus federal income tax plus state income tax if we're in one of those states, and once we start doing it automatically the tax anxiety disappears because we know the money's there when quarterly payments come due. The freelancers who get destroyed by taxes are usually the ones who spent everything as it came in and then discovered they owed five figures with nothing saved, which creates a hole that takes years to climb out of because now we're paying last year's taxes while trying to save for this year's taxes while also trying to cover regular living expenses.

Building an emergency fund matters more for freelancers than for almost anyone else because we have zero safety net beyond what we create ourselves, no unemployment benefits if clients dry up, no paid sick leave if we get too ill to work, nothing but whatever cash we managed to save before things went wrong. Employees can get by with three months of expenses saved because worst case they get laid off and collect unemployment while job hunting, but we need closer to six or twelve months because when our income drops to zero it stays there until we find new clients and complete new projects and wait for those new clients to actually pay their invoices, which could easily be four months start to finish even if we're hustling hard the whole time.

The emergency fund also needs to be separate from the buffer fund we use to smooth out monthly income variations, because those are two different things serving different purposes and mixing them means we'll drain our emergency money dealing with normal slow months instead of saving it for actual emergencies. The buffer holds two or three months of expenses and gets used regularly, money flowing in during good months and flowing out during slow months, keeping our self-salary consistent even when business income isn't. The emergency fund holds six to twelve months and sits there untouched unless something truly bad happens, like a major client suddenly canceling a retainer or a health issue that stops us from working for an extended period.

Getting all of this set up takes about ninety days if we're being realistic about the timeline, and pretending we can fix years of financial chaos in two weeks just sets us up for failure and disappointment when it doesn't magically work overnight. The first month is mostly assessment and setup, gathering our actual income and expense data from the past six months or a year, calculating our real baseline costs, opening the right bank accounts, choosing accounting software that doesn't make us want to quit entirely. The second month is implementation, actually starting to pay ourselves that consistent salary, making our first automatic transfers to tax savings, tracking every dollar that moves so we can see patterns we've been missing. The third month is refinement, comparing what actually happened to what we planned, adjusting the numbers based on reality instead of optimistic estimates, fixing the parts that didn't work as well as we hoped.

After those first ninety days we'll have a system that actually functions instead of just theory about how things should work, and that system gets stronger every month as we keep using it and making small adjustments based on what we learn. Six months in we should have a decent emergency fund started and our tax savings on track, no more panic about quarterly payments or unexpected bills. A year in we've probably weathered at least one genuinely slow period without going into debt or freaking out, which proves the system works and gives us confidence that we can actually handle this freelance life long term.

None of this is complicated in the sense that it requires advanced math or financial expertise, but it does require actually doing things differently than we've been doing them, which is harder than it sounds because our current habits are deeply ingrained even when those habits aren't serving us. The freelancer who's been mixing business and personal money in one checking account for three years will find it genuinely difficult to start using separate accounts even though intellectually they know it's better, simply because the old way is automatic and the new way requires thinking about it every single time until it becomes automatic too.

What makes this all worth the effort is the shift from constantly worrying about money to having a system we trust, from checking our bank balance five times a day hoping it magically increased to knowing exactly where we stand because we reviewed everything last Sunday and nothing significant has changed since then. Financial stability as a freelancer doesn't mean our income stops varying, it means we've built systems that handle the variation without creating constant stress, and those systems work whether we're having our best month ever or our slowest month in a year because they're designed for variability instead of fighting against it.

The freelancers who make this work aren't necessarily earning more than the ones who struggle, they've just put better systems in place, and those systems can be built by anyone willing to spend ninety days actually implementing them instead of just reading about how nice it would be to have financial stability someday. We're not aiming for perfect here, we're aiming for functional and sustainable, something that works well enough that we can focus on our actual work instead of constantly managing financial crises that shouldn't exist in the first place.

Everything that follows breaks down exactly how to build these systems step by step, with real numbers from real freelancers so we can see what this looks like in practice instead of just theory, and the assumption throughout is that we're smart capable people who just need better information about how to handle the specific financial challenges that come with irregular income. No motivation speeches, no shame about past mistakes, just practical information about what works and why it works and how to actually make it happen starting this week instead of someday when conditions are perfect, because conditions will never be perfect and waiting for them to be perfect is just another way of avoiding the uncomfortable work of changing our financial habits.

Getting started means picking one thing from the next chapter and actually doing it, not reading the whole book and then doing nothing because we're overwhelmed by how much needs to change. One thing this week, another thing next week, steady progress over ninety days that adds up to a completely different financial reality by the time we hit that three-month mark. The transformation isn't dramatic in any single week, but comparing where we are ninety days from now to where we are right now will make it obvious that something fundamental shifted, and that shift is what lets us stop living invoice to invoice and start building actual financial security despite the inherent uncertainty of freelance work.

Where Our Money Actually Goes

Tracking our expenses for sixty days straight feels like the most boring assignment anyone could possibly give us, right up there with watching paint dry or reading terms of service agreements, but the gap between what we think we spend and what we actually spend is usually so massive that those two months of tedious record-keeping end up being worth more than any other financial advice we'll ever get. We're convinced we know where our money goes because we pay rent and buy groceries and fill up the gas tank, but ask us exactly how much we spent on food last month or how much those random Amazon purchases added up to and most of us are guessing within a few hundred dollars either direction, which doesn't sound like much until we realize we're making these guesses while trying to build a budget that's supposed to guide our entire financial life.

The resistance to tracking comes partly from fear of what we'll find, because deep down we suspect we're spending more than we should on things that don't really matter, and seeing the actual numbers means we can't pretend anymore that we're being responsible when we're really just hoping everything works out. But the other part of the resistance is that tracking feels like punishment, like we're putting ourselves under surveillance because we can't be trusted, when actually tracking is just gathering data so we can make informed decisions instead of operating on vibes and optimistic assumptions that rarely match reality.

Starting the tracking process doesn't require fancy apps or complicated systems, though those exist if we want them later. For the first sixty days we can get by with a simple spreadsheet or even a notebook where we write down every single thing we spend money on, the amount, the date, and what it was for. This sounds insane when we first start doing it because who wants to log a three dollar coffee or a twelve dollar lunch, but those small purchases are usually where huge amounts of money disappear without us noticing because none of them feel significant enough to remember or worry about.

Bank statements and credit card statements give us most of what we need if we're willing to actually read through them line by line instead of just checking the total and moving on, but they miss cash purchases and they don't always make it obvious what a transaction was actually for when the merchant name is some cryptic abbreviation. Going through two months of statements takes maybe three hours total, less time than we'll waste scrolling social media this week, and what we learn from those three hours shapes every financial decision we make going forward because suddenly we're working with facts instead of feelings.

The categories that matter most for freelancers are different from what matters for employees, because we've got business expenses mixed in with personal expenses even if we're trying to keep them separate, and we need to see both clearly to understand what's really happening with our money. Personal fixed expenses include rent or mortgage, insurance premiums for health and car and renters or homeowners, subscriptions we pay monthly like streaming services or software, utilities that vary slightly but stay in a predictable range, and minimum debt payments if we're carrying any. Personal variable expenses cover groceries and gas, eating out and entertainment, clothing and household items, medical costs beyond insurance, and all those miscellaneous purchases that add up faster than we expect.

Business fixed expenses show up as software subscriptions we need for work, website hosting and domain renewals, professional memberships or associations, business insurance if we have it, and accounting or legal fees if we're paying someone to handle those. Business variable expenses include equipment and supplies we buy as needed, marketing and advertising costs that fluctuate based on how busy we are, professional development like courses or conferences, travel for business purposes, and client entertainment or meals that we can deduct at fifty percent.

Then there are the expenses we always forget until they hit us, the ones that only come up once or twice a year but still need to get paid, and these are the ones that destroy budgets because we never account for them in our monthly planning. Annual insurance premiums get paid all at once instead of monthly, professional licenses and certifications need renewing, software we pay yearly for instead of monthly suddenly charges us two hundred dollars, estimated quarterly taxes come due four times a year, and holiday spending spikes every December whether we planned for it or not.

Going through sixty days of actual spending reveals patterns we didn't know existed, like how we always order takeout on Tuesdays because that's when we're tired from back-to-back client calls, or how we spend way more in months when we're stressed about money because shopping makes us feel better temporarily even though it makes the problem worse. We might discover we're paying for three different streaming services we barely use, or that coffee shops are costing us a hundred and fifty a month when we thought it was maybe fifty, or that those small app purchases for games or productivity tools have added up to eighty dollars we didn't know we spent.

The subscriptions are usually the biggest surprise because we signed up thinking we'd use something all the time and then forgot it was charging us fifteen dollars a month for the past two years, and when we multiply fifteen by twenty-four months we realize we just found three hundred and sixty dollars we can redirect toward something that actually matters. We're not saying cut everything we enjoy, we're saying cut the things we're paying for but not actually using, because there's no point funding services that aren't improving our lives just because we can't be bothered to cancel them.

Most freelancers find they're spending somewhere between twenty and forty percent more than they estimated before tracking, which explains why we always feel broke despite earning what should be enough. If we think our essential expenses are three thousand a month but they're actually four thousand, we need to earn a lot more to feel secure, and we've been operating under the wrong assumption about our baseline which means every financial plan we've made has been built on faulty numbers. Fixing this doesn't mean we need to immediately cut spending by a thousand dollars, though we might find easy cuts once we see where money's going, it means we need to know the real number so we can earn enough to cover it and build savings on top of it.

Calculating our baseline from two months of actual data means adding up everything we truly can't skip, not everything we currently spend but everything we absolutely have to spend to maintain basic functioning. Rent or mortgage goes in the baseline because we need somewhere to live, but restaurants and entertainment don't go in the baseline even if we currently spend money there every month. Health insurance goes in the baseline, gym memberships probably don't unless exercise is genuinely critical to our mental or physical health and we actually use the gym regularly instead of paying for motivation we never act on.

The baseline number tells us the absolute minimum we need to earn and keep every month to avoid going into debt or missing payments, and for most freelancers this ends up being somewhere between sixty and eighty percent of their current total spending because the other twenty to forty percent is discretionary even if it doesn't feel discretionary when we're doing it. Someone spending five thousand a month might have a baseline of three thousand five hundred, which means if income drops below that they need to cut discretionary spending or pull from savings, but as long as they're hitting that thirty-five hundred they can cover the essentials without crisis.

Knowing our baseline also shows us how much buffer we need to build, because the buffer needs to hold two or three months of baseline expenses, not two or three months of total spending including everything we could theoretically cut if we had to. If our baseline is three thousand five hundred, a three-month buffer is ten thousand five hundred, which is a lot more achievable than a three-month buffer based on five thousand monthly spending which would be fifteen thousand. We're still going to build toward covering our full spending eventually, but starting with baseline makes the goal feel possible instead of impossible.

The other thing tracking reveals is seasonal patterns we knew about vaguely but never actually quantified, like how we spend way more on gas in summer when we're driving to visit family or clients, or how winter utility bills are double what they are in spring, or how we always buy new equipment in January when we're motivated to improve our business setup. These patterns mean our monthly expenses aren't actually consistent even when we think they are, and planning for a flat three thousand every month sets us up for failure when some months are really thirty-five hundred and others are twenty-five hundred.

Looking at seasonal patterns over a full year, if we have that much history, helps us understand when to expect higher expenses and when we'll have breathing room, which matters for planning when to take vacations or when to push harder on client acquisition. If we know October through December are slow for income but busy for spending because of holidays, we can plan to build up cash during the summer instead of spending everything we earn in June and July just because it's available.

Real example from a freelance writer earning between three and seven thousand monthly shows baseline expenses of twenty-eight hundred covering rent at fourteen hundred, health insurance at three hundred, car insurance and gas at two-fifty total, groceries at four hundred, utilities averaging one-fifty, phone at sixty, and student loan minimum at two hundred forty. Variable spending on top of that runs another twelve to eighteen hundred depending on the month, including eating out, entertainment, clothing, household items, and discretionary purchases. Business expenses add roughly five hundred monthly for software subscriptions, occasional equipment, professional development, and supplies.

That writer thought they needed about four thousand monthly to feel comfortable, but the real baseline is only twenty-eight hundred, which means months earning thirty-five hundred leave seven hundred for variable spending and savings even though that's below the typical income. The months earning six or seven thousand suddenly have three or four thousand available for buffer building, emergency fund, retirement, and increased variable spending, instead of just disappearing into general expenses without a clear purpose.

Another example from a graphic designer shows baseline of thirty-two hundred including rent at sixteen hundred, health insurance at four hundred, car payment at three-fifty, car insurance at one hundred, utilities at two hundred, groceries at four hundred, and minimum credit card payment at one-fifty. Business expenses average six hundred monthly for Adobe Creative Cloud, website hosting, stock image subscriptions, and occasional fonts or plugins. Variable personal spending runs ten to fifteen hundred depending on how stressed the designer is, because stress shopping is real and tracking made that pattern obvious.

The designer's income ranges from four thousand to nine thousand monthly, averaging about six thousand, which seems like plenty until we realize baseline plus business expenses is thirty-eight hundred and typical total spending hits fifty-five hundred, leaving only five hundred monthly for savings and buffer building even at average income. The months below average mean pulling from savings or going into credit card debt, which explains why the designer never felt like they were getting ahead despite earning seventy-two thousand annually.

Tracking also reveals the expenses that sneak up because we don't think about them as regular costs even though they happen predictably. Domain renewals hit once a year, usually right when we've forgotten about them. Annual subscriptions for tools we use daily come due all at once instead of spreading across months. Professional liability insurance renews annually. Accounting fees for tax prep happen every April. Conference tickets and travel might happen twice a year. Each one alone isn't budget-breaking, but add them all together and suddenly we need an extra two thousand in March and another fifteen hundred in October, and if we didn't plan for that we're either going into debt or raiding the emergency fund for non-emergencies.

The solution is calculating these annual or quarterly expenses, dividing them across twelve months, and including that monthly amount in our budget even though we're not spending it every month, setting it aside in savings until the actual bill comes due. If annual expenses total six thousand, that's five hundred monthly we need to account for, bringing it from invisible expense that attacks randomly to planned expense we're ready for.

Some freelancers resist tracking this thoroughly because they think knowing exactly where money goes will make them feel restricted or judged, like they'll have to defend every purchase to themselves or cut out everything fun to meet some arbitrary standard. But tracking isn't about judgment, it's about awareness, and awareness gives us power to make intentional choices instead of drifting through months wondering where thousands of dollars disappeared.

We can still spend money on things we enjoy, we just know we're doing it and can decide if that purchase is worth more than whatever else we could do with that money. A hundred dollars on concerts might be completely worth it because live music brings genuine joy, while a hundred dollars on streaming services we barely use might be money we'd rather have in savings. Neither choice is wrong, but one is intentional and one is just default behavior we never examined.

The tracking period ends after sixty days, but the awareness we gain from it continues forever because now we know how to look at our spending critically instead of just hoping everything works out. We don't necessarily track every purchase forever, though some people find they prefer it, but we do check in monthly to make sure spending is roughly where we expect it to be and nothing weird is happening that we haven't noticed.

Those two months of detailed tracking give us the baseline number we'll use for everything that comes next, the self-salary we'll pay ourselves, the buffer we'll build, the emergency fund we'll target, and the income we need to earn consistently to make this whole freelance thing sustainable instead of constantly stressful. Without accurate baseline numbers we're just guessing, and guessing means we're either being too conservative and making ourselves miserable by underspending, or too optimistic and setting ourselves up for the same financial chaos we're trying to escape.

Starting the tracking this week instead of putting it off until next month or after this busy period or when things calm down means we'll have real data in eight weeks, and real data beats perfect conditions every single time.

Understanding Our Real Income

The freelancer who says they make five thousand a month is probably averaging that over the past six months, which means some months they made eight thousand and others they made two thousand, and treating those wildly different months as equivalent creates all kinds of problems when we're trying to plan our financial lives. The employee making five thousand actually gets five thousand on the first and fifteenth like clockwork, so their planning is simple, but our planning needs to account for the fact that next month's income could be anywhere in a three or four thousand dollar range and we won't know which end of that range until invoices actually get paid.

Most of us started freelancing with optimistic ideas about steady income growth, thinking we'd land a few good clients and then coast on reliable retainer work that shows up every month without fail, but the reality is that even retainer clients sometimes pause projects or reduce hours or disappear entirely when their budget changes, and project work is inherently lumpy because we're either working on something or we're not. The months we're heads down finishing three projects simultaneously bring in great money, then we deliver everything and suddenly we're in a gap waiting for new projects to start, and that gap might be two weeks or it might be two months depending on how fast new clients move through their decision making process.

Understanding our real income means looking at the past six to twelve months and seeing both the average and the range, because the average tells us what we typically make but the range tells us what we need to be prepared for. A freelancer averaging six thousand monthly with a range of four to eight thousand faces different planning challenges than one averaging six thousand with a range of five to seven thousand, even though both are making the same total annual income. The wider the range, the more buffer we need and the more conservative we should be with our baseline planning number.

Calculating average monthly income over six months means adding up everything we earned in those six months and dividing by six, which gives us a number we can use for general planning even though no individual month probably hit that exact number. A freelancer who earned five thousand, seven thousand, three thousand, eight thousand, four thousand, and six thousand over the past half year has a total of thirty-three thousand, divided by six gives fifty-five hundred average, but notice how only one month actually hit that fifty-five hundred number and the others were all either well above or well below.

Using twelve months instead of six gives us a more stable average that accounts for seasonal patterns, because many freelance industries have busy and slow seasons that repeat annually but get masked when we're only looking at a short period. The writer who does a lot of corporate blog work might see slow summers when companies are focused on other things and busy falls when everyone's trying to hit year-end goals. The designer doing holiday campaign work gets slammed September through November and then hits a wall in January when nobody's spending on marketing after the holiday push.

Looking at twelve months of income also helps us spot whether we're trending up, trending down, or staying stable, which matters for planning because growing income means we can be slightly more aggressive with our planning numbers while declining income means we need to be more conservative and probably spend some energy on client acquisition. The freelancer whose income has grown from four thousand to seven thousand over twelve months has different momentum than the one whose income has dropped from seven thousand to four thousand, and pretending those situations are the same because the average works out similar is setting ourselves up for trouble.

Real example from a web developer shows monthly income over twelve months of forty-five hundred, six thousand, seven thousand five hundred, eight thousand, six thousand five hundred, five thousand, four thousand, nine thousand, seven thousand, five thousand five hundred, six thousand, and eight thousand. Total for the year is seventy-seven thousand, divided by twelve gives sixty-four hundred monthly average, but the range runs from four thousand to nine thousand, which is a five thousand dollar spread that makes planning based on the average pretty risky.

That developer can't safely budget assuming sixty-four hundred will show up every month, because four of those twelve months came in below that number, and if we're budgeting based on money we might not actually receive we're setting ourselves up for the same stress we're trying to eliminate. The better approach for someone with that much variability is using either the lowest recent month or some conservative number between the lowest month and the average, accepting that we'll have extra money during good months but we won't be scrambling during slow months.

The lowest month method means looking at the past six or twelve months, finding the smallest amount we earned in any of those months, and using that as our planning income for budgeting purposes. It's conservative to the point of feeling almost too careful, but being too careful beats being too optimistic when we're talking about whether we can pay rent. For the developer whose lowest month was four thousand, planning around four thousand means every other month brings extra money that can go toward buffer building, emergency fund, or getting ahead on expenses.

Some freelancers resist this approach because it feels like we're planning to fail or expecting the worst, but actually we're just planning for reality, and reality includes the fact that slow months happen and we can't predict exactly when they'll hit. Planning for the best case means we're constantly disappointed and stressed when average months feel like failure because they're not as good as our optimistic projection. Planning for something closer to the worst case means most months feel like wins because we did better than expected.

The math for lowest-month planning is simple once we accept the mental shift it requires. Take the past six months of income, identify the smallest number, and that becomes our baseline planning income. If we want to be slightly less conservative we can average the three lowest months instead of using just the absolute lowest, which gives us a number that's still safe but not quite as tight. The developer with months of four thousand, four thousand five hundred, five thousand, five thousand five hundred, six thousand, and six thousand five hundred would use four thousand for maximum safety or forty-seven hundred for the three-month-low average.

The difference between planning on four thousand versus sixty-four hundred is massive in terms of financial stress, because planning on four thousand means we build our self-salary and our budget around that number, and then when we earn sixty-four hundred we have twenty-four hundred extra that month that goes toward getting ahead instead of just covering baseline expenses. Planning on sixty-four hundred means months we only earn four thousand create a twenty-four hundred shortfall we have to cover somehow, usually by pulling from savings or putting expenses on credit cards, which defeats the whole purpose of trying to build financial stability.

Finding our planning income also requires understanding how our actual income timing works, because the money we earned this month might not hit our account until next month or even the month after depending on client payment terms. A project we finished and invoiced on March 15th with net-thirty terms doesn't get paid until April 15th at best, and if the client takes forty-five days like many do, that payment shows up in early May. This timing gap means we need to think about cash flow separately from work completed, because we might have a great month in terms of projects finished but a terrible month in terms of money actually received.

Tracking both the work we complete and the payments we receive helps us understand the lag between effort and income, and that lag is usually where cash flow problems hide. The freelancer who lands three great projects in January and finishes them all by February might think they're crushing it until they realize none of those invoices will get paid until March or April, leaving them with two months of low income despite high productivity. Building enough buffer to cover this lag means we're not constantly stressed about whether this week's invoice will get paid in time to cover next week's rent.

Income patterns worth spotting include the obvious seasonal ones where certain times of year are reliably busier than others, but also the less obvious patterns around client behavior and project types. Some clients always pay within ten days regardless of stated terms, making them more valuable for cash flow even if their projects pay the same as clients who take fifty days. Some types of projects, like ongoing retainers, provide more predictable income than one-off projects even if the total annual income is similar, and adjusting our client mix toward more predictable work can smooth out the variability even if it doesn't increase total earnings.

Retainer income versus project income creates very different planning situations because retainers give us a baseline we can count on each month even though they might not be our entire income. The freelancer with two thousand in monthly retainers and three to five thousand in project work has a floor of two thousand they can plan around, making budgeting easier than the freelancer with zero retainers and two to seven thousand in pure project work. Both might average the same annually, but the one with retainers has more stability and less stress about covering baseline expenses.

Long-term trends matter because we need to know if we're growing, stable, or declining, and that knowledge shapes how aggressively we can plan for the future. The freelancer whose income has grown twenty percent over the past year can probably plan slightly above their current average, while the freelancer whose income has dropped twenty percent needs to plan conservatively and focus energy on fixing whatever caused the decline. Pretending the trend doesn't exist or assuming it'll reverse itself without action is how we end up in financial crisis.

Real example from a freelance photographer shows clear seasonal patterns where summer wedding season brings eight to twelve thousand monthly, fall brings five to seven thousand, winter drops to three to four thousand, and spring climbs back to six to eight thousand. The annual average works out to about seventy-five thousand or sixty-three hundred monthly, but planning based on that average means summer looks like extra money months and winter feels like failure months, when actually they're just predictable seasonal variation the photographer should plan for.

Better approach for that photographer is recognizing the pattern and building budget around the winter low of three to four thousand, knowing that summer surplus of four to eight thousand extra gets saved to carry through the next winter. This eliminates the stress of wondering how to cover expenses in December and January because the money was already set aside in June and July when income was high. Fighting the seasonal pattern by trying to market harder in winter to bring income up rarely works as well as accepting the pattern and planning around it.

Another example from a freelance consultant shows a different pattern where income is relatively stable month to month at five to seven thousand, but once or twice a year a large project brings in fifteen to twenty thousand in a single month. The annual average including those spikes is close to ninety thousand or seventy-five hundred monthly, but planning around seventy-five hundred doesn't make sense when most months are actually closer to six thousand and the large payments are unpredictable bonuses rather than reliable income.

That consultant should plan around six thousand as the reliable monthly number and treat the large project payments as buffer builders and emergency fund deposits rather than regular income to budget against. The mental shift required here is seeing those big payments as opportunities to get ahead rather than as money we can spend on upgrading our lifestyle, because lifestyle upgrades based on occasional spikes in income mean we're constantly stressed during normal months trying to maintain that upgraded lifestyle on lower regular income.

The calculation we're working toward is our planning income, which is the number we'll use to set our self-salary in the next chapter and build our budget around going forward. For most freelancers with significant income variability, the planning income ends up being somewhere between the lowest recent month and the average, depending on how risk-averse we are and how much buffer we've already built. Someone just starting to get their finances organized should use a more conservative number, while someone with six months of buffer and a solid emergency fund can afford to plan slightly closer to average.

Three different freelancers earning the same seventy-five thousand annually might have very different planning incomes based on their situations. The one with income ranging from four to nine thousand monthly, no buffer, and unpredictable client mix should probably plan around four to five thousand to be safe. The one with income ranging from five to eight thousand, some retainer work providing a floor, and three months of buffer built can probably plan around six thousand. The one with stable income of six to seven thousand every month, strong client relationships, and full emergency fund can plan around sixty-five hundred without much risk.

The point isn't to find the perfect number through some complex formula, it's to pick a number we're confident we can hit or exceed most months, and then build our financial life around that number instead of around optimistic projections that leave us scrambling when reality doesn't cooperate. Conservative planning doesn't mean we're expecting to fail or being negative about our business, it means we're building financial stability that can weather the inevitable slow periods without creating crisis.

Some freelancers get uncomfortable with this exercise because looking closely at their income patterns reveals that they're not actually making as much as they thought they were, or that their income has been declining and they've been pretending not to notice, or that they have way more variability than feels safe. That discomfort is useful information rather than something to avoid, because we can't fix problems we're pretending don't exist, and financial problems don't get better when we ignore them.

The freelancer who realizes their income has been trending down for six months needs that information so they can focus energy on client acquisition, raise rates, or adjust their business model before things get worse. The freelancer who sees that their income swings wildly month to month might decide to focus on landing more retainer clients to create stability even if it means slightly lower total income. The freelancer who discovers most of their income comes from one or two clients understands they need to diversify before one of those clients disappears and tanks their entire income overnight.

Understanding our real income also means accepting that the number might change over time and we need to revisit this calculation every six months or so to make sure our planning income still matches reality. The business that was averaging six thousand monthly last year might be averaging eight thousand now after landing better clients and raising rates, which means we can adjust our planning income upward and increase our self-salary. The business that was stable at seven thousand might have dropped to five thousand after losing a major client, which means we need to adjust planning income down and either cut expenses or hustle harder to replace that lost income.

The goal isn't perfection in predicting exactly what we'll earn each month, because that's impossible with irregular income, but rather having a realistic sense of what we can count on so we can plan accordingly. Once we know our planning income and our baseline expenses from the previous chapter, we can see clearly whether we're earning enough to cover our baseline with room for savings, or whether we're in a situation where our expenses exceed our reliable income and we need to either earn more or spend less to avoid slow financial decline into debt.

That clarity might be uncomfortable if the numbers aren't what we hoped, but clarity beats confusion every single time when we're trying to build financial stability.

The Self-Salary System

Paying ourselves a consistent amount every month regardless of what clients actually paid us sounds impossible until we understand that we're not trying to make our business income consistent, we're just creating a consistent transfer from business income to personal spending, and those are completely different things. The business account can have wild swings where fifteen thousand shows up one month and three thousand the next, but our personal account receives the same forty-five hundred every single month because we're smoothing out those swings before the money reaches our day-to-day life.

This separation between business money and personal money changes everything about how we experience financial stress, because suddenly we're not checking the business account balance and panicking about whether we can pay rent, we're checking our personal account which has the predictable salary we just paid ourselves and budgeting becomes simple again. The chaos stays contained in the business account where we can handle it strategically instead of letting it spill into our personal finances and create constant anxiety about basic expenses.

Setting up two separate bank accounts seems like extra work when we're already busy running the business and doing client work, but the mental clarity it creates is worth way more than the fifteen minutes it takes to open a second account and link them together. Most freelancers who resist this separation are unconsciously trying to avoid seeing clearly how their business is actually performing, because when everything's mixed together in one account we can pretend things are fine even when they're not, but once we separate business and personal the numbers become impossible to ignore.

The business account holds all client payments when they arrive, all business expenses get paid from this account, and at the designated time each month we transfer our salary to the personal account. That's it. Three simple rules that create complete financial clarity where before we had confusion and stress. Client pays an invoice, money goes to business account. We need to buy software for work, money comes from business account. First of the month arrives, we transfer our predetermined salary amount to personal account and pay ourselves just like an employer would.

Opening a business account doesn't require having an LLC or any formal business structure, though some banks prefer it and offer better features if we do. As a sole proprietor we can open a business account using our Social Security number instead of an EIN, though getting an EIN from the IRS takes about five minutes online and makes everything slightly more professional. The important thing is having an account that's clearly designated for business use and completely separate from our personal checking and savings.

The features that matter in a business account are pretty basic for most freelancers because we're not running a huge operation with payroll and complex transactions. We need free or low-cost monthly fees, ideally zero because paying twenty dollars a month just to have an account seems wasteful when free options exist. We need easy transfers to our personal account without fees or restrictions. We need mobile deposit for client checks if we still get any of those. We need integration with whatever accounting software we choose so transactions flow automatically instead of requiring manual entry.

Banks built specifically for freelancers like Found offer features designed for our situation, including automatic tax savings and expense categorization, which can be worth using even if the account itself isn't perfect in other ways. Traditional banks like Chase or Bank of America offer business accounts that work fine and have the advantage of physical branches if we prefer in-person banking for certain things. Online banks like Axos or Novo tend to have fewer fees and better interest rates but no physical locations, which matters or doesn't depending on how we prefer to bank.

The personal account can be whatever we're already using or a new account if we want a fresh start, but it needs to be completely separate from the business account with no business transactions running through it at all. Every dollar that goes into the personal account is personal money we're allowed to spend on our life, and every dollar in the business account is business money that either pays for business expenses or eventually becomes our salary. Mixing them even occasionally defeats the purpose because then we're back to not knowing whether that five thousand in our account is money we can spend on rent and groceries or money we need to cover the annual software renewal next week.

Setting up the accounts means going to the bank's website or app, clicking through the new account process, answering questions about what kind of account we want and how we'll use it, and waiting a few days for everything to get approved and activated. Some banks want to see business documents or proof of business activity, others are fine with just our word that we're freelancing. The whole process takes maybe thirty minutes of actual work spread across a few days of waiting for approvals.

Linking the two accounts so we can transfer between them is usually just providing the routing and account numbers for each account in the other account's settings, though some banks make us verify small test deposits to prove we own both accounts. Once linked, transfers between them should be instant or at most next-day, because waiting three to five business days to pay ourselves would defeat the purpose of having consistent cash flow.

Calculating our monthly salary starts with the baseline expenses we figured out in chapter one and the planning income we determined in chapter two, and the relationship between those numbers tells us how much we can safely pay ourselves. If our baseline is thirty-five hundred and our planning income is fifty-five hundred, we have two thousand of margin to work with, which needs to cover tax savings, emergency fund building, buffer creation, and any variable spending beyond baseline.

The conservative approach is setting salary at or just above baseline, leaving all the margin in the business account to build buffer and cover the variability we know is coming. If baseline is thirty-five hundred, we might set salary at thirty-seven hundred, giving ourselves a tiny bit of breathing room but keeping most of the margin in business to handle months when income drops below planning level. This feels restrictive at first, especially during good months when the business account is flush with cash and we're only taking out thirty-seven hundred, but it builds financial stability faster than any other approach.

The moderate approach is setting salary somewhere between baseline and planning income, maybe splitting the difference. With thirty-five hundred baseline and fifty-five hundred planning income, we might set salary at forty-five hundred, giving ourselves an extra thousand beyond baseline for variable spending and small luxuries, while keeping a thousand in business each month to build buffer. This works once we've got some buffer already established, but starting here before we have any cushion means we're taking more risk than we probably should.

The aggressive approach is setting salary close to planning income and trusting that we'll earn at least that much most months, which might work for someone with very stable income despite being technically freelance, but puts us right back in the stressful position of wondering if this month's income will cover the salary we're expecting to pay ourselves. For most freelancers with typical variability, the aggressive approach is just setting ourselves up for the same problems we're trying to solve.

Real example with actual numbers shows a freelancer with baseline expenses of forty-two hundred and planning income of sixty-three hundred based on twelve months of history ranging from forty-five hundred to eight thousand monthly. The margin between baseline and planning income is two thousand, which needs to cover taxes at thirty percent of gross income, buffer building, emergency fund deposits, and variable spending beyond baseline.

Tax savings on sixty-three hundred income is about nineteen hundred monthly, leaving only a hundred dollars of that two thousand margin for everything else, which clearly doesn't work. This is where we discover that our planning income isn't actually high enough to cover our baseline expenses plus taxes plus savings, and we need to either increase income, decrease baseline expenses, or accept that we're not going to build savings as fast as we'd like until income grows.

That freelancer decides to set salary at baseline of forty-two hundred, keep the full nineteen hundred for taxes automatically, and anything above seventy-three hundred gross income in a month gets split between buffer building and emergency fund. Months earning the planning income of sixty-three hundred mean paying forty-two hundred salary, saving nineteen hundred for taxes, leaving six hundred that stays in business to slowly build buffer. Months earning eight thousand mean paying forty-two hundred salary, saving twenty-four hundred for taxes, leaving thirteen hundred for buffer and emergency fund.

Another example with more margin shows a freelancer with baseline of three thousand and planning income of six thousand, creating three thousand of margin. Tax savings on six thousand is eighteen hundred, leaving twelve hundred for buffer, emergency fund, and variable spending. This freelancer sets salary at thirty-five hundred, giving themselves five hundred beyond baseline for discretionary spending, while reserving the other seven hundred of margin for savings and buffer building after taxes.

The salary we set isn't permanent, we can adjust it every few months as our situation changes, but we shouldn't adjust it constantly based on individual good or bad months because that defeats the purpose of creating consistency. Review salary every quarter, check whether planning income still matches reality and whether baseline expenses have changed, adjust if needed but otherwise stick with the number we chose.

The transfer schedule matters more than we might think because timing affects how we experience cash flow even when the total amounts are the same. Paying ourselves on the first of every month works well if most of our major bills are due early in the month, giving us the cash to cover them right when needed. Paying ourselves on the fifteenth might work better if rent isn't due until mid-month and we prefer having the money arrive closer to when we'll spend it.

Some freelancers prefer weekly transfers of one-quarter their monthly salary, which creates even more consistency and helps if cash flow is tight, though it requires more active management. The web developer paying themselves forty-eight hundred monthly might do twelve hundred every Monday, which means they always have cash coming in and never waiting three weeks between payments feeling like money is tight even though it's not.

During lean months when business income is below our salary amount, we're pulling from the buffer we built during good months, which is exactly what the buffer is for and not something to stress about as long as buffer isn't hitting zero. If we set things up correctly with salary at or near baseline and planning income conservative enough to be reliable, lean months should be occasional rather than constant, and buffer should rebuild during the next good month without requiring any special action.

During flush months when business income is well above planning level, the extra money stays in the business account and becomes buffer automatically, which is the system working exactly as designed. We don't increase our salary just because we had a great month, we keep salary consistent and let buffer grow so it can protect us during the next slow period. The temptation to treat good months as bonus time and spend extra is strong, but giving in to that temptation means we're back to the income-to-income cycle instead of building stability.

The buffer account is technically just the business checking account with enough money sitting in it to cover our salary during months when income is low, but some freelancers prefer having a separate savings account they designate as buffer and transferring money there during good months to make the separation more visible. Either approach works as long as the money is accessible without penalties when we need it, because buffer needs to be available immediately unlike long-term savings that can sit in less accessible accounts earning slightly higher interest.

Building buffer from zero to three months of salary takes time that depends entirely on how much margin exists between our planning income and our actual expenses including salary and taxes. The freelancer with only a few hundred dollars of margin per month at planning income needs longer to build buffer than the freelancer with two thousand of margin, which is just math and not something to feel bad about, it's information about whether we need to increase income or whether we can keep building steadily.

Three months of buffer for someone paying themselves forty-five hundred monthly means having thirteen thousand five hundred sitting in the business account, which sounds like a lot until we remember that this money is protecting us from income variability and eliminating the stress of wondering whether we can pay ourselves next month. The freelancer earning sixty-five hundred planning income with a thousand of margin after salary and taxes needs about fourteen months to build that buffer, which is a long time but still better than never building it and staying in constant financial stress.

Real timeline for a freelancer building from zero buffer shows month one with salary set at baseline of thirty-eight hundred, planning income actually coming in at fifty-five hundred, taxes of sixteen-fifty saved, leaving five hundred for buffer. Month two brings in forty-five hundred income which is below planning but still above salary, allowing normal salary payment of thirty-eight hundred, taxes of thirteen-fifty, leaving two hundred for buffer. Month three brings seven thousand, salary stays thirty-eight hundred, taxes are twenty-one hundred, buffer gets fifteen hundred.

After three months that freelancer has twenty-two hundred in buffer, about half of one month's salary, which isn't much but it's infinitely better than the zero buffer they started with. After six months of similar patterns they might have five or six thousand buffered, getting closer to two months. After a year they're hopefully at or near the full three months of buffer, which means they can weather a slow period without stress and start thinking about building emergency fund more aggressively.

The designer building buffer over eight months shows a different pattern where some months add significant buffer and other months add almost nothing, but the general trend is upward as long as income stays at or above planning level more often than below. Month one adds eight hundred, month two adds three hundred, month three adds fifteen hundred, month four adds two hundred, month five adds twelve hundred, month six adds four hundred, month seven adds eighteen hundred, month eight adds nine hundred. Total after eight months is seventy-one hundred, about six weeks of salary buffered, not the full three months yet but getting there.

The psychological shift that happens once buffer exists is massive compared to the relatively simple financial change, because suddenly we're not worried about next month even if this month was slow. We know the buffer is there, we know we can pay ourselves our salary regardless of whether new client payments arrive this week, and that knowledge eliminates the low-level constant anxiety that colored every day when we were living invoice to invoice.

Some freelancers feel guilty about money sitting in the business account "doing nothing" when it could be earning interest somewhere or getting invested, but buffer money isn't doing nothing, it's buying us peace of mind and financial stability, which has value that can't be measured in interest rates. Once buffer is fully built we can start thinking about where to keep longer-term savings for better returns, but buffer itself needs to stay liquid and accessible.

The system works best when we set it up and then mostly forget about it, checking monthly that salary got transferred and buffer level is reasonable, but not obsessing over every fluctuation in business account balance. The whole point is creating consistency in our personal finances despite inconsistency in business income, and the more we automate and systematize this process the less mental energy it requires, leaving us free to focus on actual work instead of constantly managing financial stress.

Starting this system this week means opening the business account if we don't have one yet, calculating our salary based on baseline and planning income, and making our first transfer, even if buffer doesn't exist yet and we're starting from a position of the business account being basically empty. We build buffer over time through the process of using this system, not before we start using it, and waiting until we have buffer before implementing the self-salary system means we'll never actually start because there's always a reason to wait one more month.

Budgeting How-to's

The zero-sum budget sounds complicated until we realize it just means every dollar that comes in gets assigned a specific job before we spend it, so at the end of the month our income minus all our planned expenses including savings equals zero, which doesn't mean we spent everything, it means we planned for everything. Traditional budgeting tells us to track what we spent and compare it to what we planned to spend, hoping the numbers match, but zero-sum budgeting flips this around by deciding what every dollar will do the moment it arrives, which creates way more control especially when income varies month to month.

The system works by taking whatever income we have this month, whether that's three thousand or seven thousand, and immediately dividing it into categories that represent all our financial responsibilities and goals. Rent gets its allocation, groceries get their allocation, savings gets its allocation, everything gets deliberately assigned instead of sitting in the account waiting to be spent on whatever comes up. When we're done assigning, the unallocated amount should be zero, meaning we've given every dollar a purpose even if that purpose is sitting in savings for next month.

Setting this up starts with listing every single category of expense we have, which we should already know from the tracking we did in chapter one, plus categories for things that aren't expenses like savings and buffer building. The list might include twenty or thirty different categories depending on how detailed we want to get, but the core ones are rent or mortgage, utilities, groceries, gas, insurance, phone, internet, subscriptions, eating out, entertainment, savings, tax savings, buffer building, emergency fund, and anything else that regularly takes money.

Each category gets an amount based on either what we know we'll spend because it's a fixed bill, or what we've learned we typically spend from our tracking, or what we want to limit ourselves to spending. Rent is easy because it's the same every month. Groceries require looking at our tracking to see what we actually spend, then deciding if that's reasonable or if we want to try reducing it. Entertainment might be whatever's left after all the essential categories are funded, or it might be a specific amount we've decided is reasonable based on our income level.

When our income is the same every month this process is straightforward because we're working with the same dollar amount each time, but when income varies we need to adjust our category allocations based on what actually came in. The month we earn seven thousand allows bigger allocations for variable categories like groceries and entertainment than the month we earn four thousand, but the essential categories like rent and insurance stay the same because those bills don't change based on our income.

The modified approach for irregular income means starting with our essential baseline categories and funding those first, then working through our priorities for whatever money remains. If baseline is thirty-five hundred and we earned fifty-five hundred, we fund the thirty-five hundred in essential categories, then allocate the remaining two thousand to tax savings, buffer, emergency fund, and discretionary spending in whatever priority makes sense for our current situation.

Real example shows a freelancer earning forty-eight hundred in a particular month with baseline expenses of thirty-two hundred. First allocation goes to baseline categories covering rent at fourteen hundred, health insurance at three hundred fifty, car payment at three hundred, utilities at one-eighty, groceries at four hundred, gas at one hundred twenty, phone at sixty, and minimum debt payment at two hundred, totaling the thirty-two hundred baseline. Remaining sixteen hundred gets allocated with nine hundred to tax savings, four hundred to buffer, two hundred to emergency fund, and one hundred to discretionary spending.

The same freelancer earning sixty-five hundred the next month follows the same process, funding baseline of thirty-two hundred first, then allocating the remaining thirty-three hundred. Tax savings gets thirteen hundred, buffer gets eight hundred, emergency fund gets five hundred, and discretionary categories like eating out and entertainment get seven hundred total. Notice how the baseline stays constant but everything else scales with income, which is how we handle variability without creating budget chaos.

During months when income falls below baseline, the budget still needs to equal zero but now we're pulling from buffer to make up the difference, which requires adding a category for buffer withdrawal and treating it like negative income. If we earned twenty-eight hundred against baseline of thirty-two hundred, we withdraw four hundred from buffer, giving us effectively thirty-two hundred to work with, fund all baseline categories, and accept that nothing goes to savings this month because we're in survival mode.

The 50/30/20 rule from traditional budgeting says to spend fifty percent on needs, thirty percent on wants, and twenty percent on savings, which sounds reasonable until we try applying it to freelance life and realize it doesn't account for business expenses, taxes, or the need to build buffer. The modified version for freelancers shifts those percentages to fifty percent for business operations plus personal salary, thirty percent for business growth and development, and twenty percent for taxes and long-term savings.

Breaking down the modified fifty percent shows it covering both business expenses we can't avoid and our personal salary we transfer to ourselves, treating that salary as the largest business expense rather than thinking of the business as separate from our personal life. For someone earning seventy-two hundred monthly, fifty percent is thirty-six hundred, which might break down as eight hundred in business expenses like software, internet, phone, supplies, insurance, with the remaining twenty-eight hundred being salary we pay ourselves.

The thirty percent for growth covers things that improve the business or our skills, like professional development courses, better equipment, marketing and advertising, networking events, and anything else that's an investment in future earning potential rather than just operational necessity. On seventy-two hundred income that's twenty-one sixty, which could be fifty dollars monthly for an online course subscription, a hundred for coworking space membership, two hundred for marketing, and the rest saved toward attending a conference next quarter or buying better camera equipment.

The twenty percent for savings covers both tax obligations we can't avoid and long-term savings we're trying to build, which is where this modified rule gets tight because twenty percent of income needs to stretch across taxes that consume at least twenty-five to thirty percent of income before we even get to emergency fund or retirement. On seventy-two hundred income, twenty percent is fourteen forty, but taxes on seventy-two hundred should be around twenty-two hundred, which means this rule doesn't actually work mathematically unless we're somehow paying much lower taxes than most freelancers.

The problem with trying to force percentages onto irregular income is that they work fine when income is high but fall apart when income is low, and rigid percentages don't account for the fact that some expenses are fixed regardless of income while others can flex. A better approach is the priority hierarchy where we fund things in order of necessity rather than by percentage, starting with absolute essentials and working down to nice-to-haves based on how much money actually showed up.

Priority one is baseline expenses that we literally can't skip without immediate crisis, things like housing, utilities, minimum food, transportation to get to work or clients, insurance, and minimum debt payments. These get funded first no matter what, even if it means we have nothing left for anything else, because losing housing or having insurance lapse creates problems that take months or years to fix.

Priority two is tax savings because even though the crisis isn't immediate, owing the IRS creates problems that snowball fast and we cannot skip tax savings except in genuine emergency situations where we have no other option. Setting aside at least twenty-five percent for taxes comes right after baseline is covered, before we spend money on anything discretionary or even on business growth.

Priority three is buffer and emergency fund building because these create the stability that makes everything else work, and skipping them means we stay trapped in the same financial stress we're trying to escape. How much goes here depends on how much buffer and emergency fund we already have, with more going to buffer when it's still being built and more going to emergency fund once buffer is solid.

Priority four covers business growth and development expenses that will increase our earning potential, which makes them more important than personal discretionary spending even though they're not as critical as baseline survival needs. We can skip the professional development course this month if money is tight, but consistently skipping all business investment means our income won't grow and we'll stay stuck at current earning levels.

Priority five is discretionary personal spending on things that make life enjoyable but aren't necessary for survival or business function, stuff like eating out, entertainment, hobbies, travel, and upgrades to things that currently work fine. This money only gets allocated after everything else is funded, which means during tight months there might be nothing here, and that's fine because we're not trying to maintain a certain lifestyle, we're trying to build financial stability.

Living on last month's income takes the zero-sum approach and adds a timing shift where we're always one month ahead, using January's income to fund February's budget rather than trying to budget January's income during January when we don't know yet how much will actually come in. This eliminates the guessing game entirely because by the time we're budgeting for February, January is over and we know exactly how much income we have to work with.

Getting one month ahead requires either having a really good month where income significantly exceeds expenses, or gradually building toward it by spending slightly less than we earn for several months until we've accumulated one month's worth of expenses in savings. For someone with baseline of thirty-five hundred, getting one month ahead means having thirty-five hundred sitting in savings ready to fund next month's baseline while this month's income can be set aside for the month after.

The transition period is the hardest part because we're simultaneously trying to cover this month's expenses with this month's income while also building up enough savings to eventually cover next month's expenses with this month's income, which feels impossible until we find ways to either increase income temporarily or decrease expenses temporarily to create the gap. Some freelancers do this by taking on extra project work for a month or two, others cut discretionary spending to bare minimum for a few months, either way it requires short-term sacrifice for long-term benefit.

Real example of getting one month ahead shows a freelancer with baseline of thirty-eight hundred and typical income of fifty-five hundred, which leaves seventeen hundred margin for taxes, savings, and discretionary. They decide to get ahead by cutting discretionary spending to almost nothing for three months, saving the full margin minus taxes, which is about seven hundred monthly after setting aside eleven hundred for taxes. After three months they have twenty-one hundred saved, not quite enough for the full thirty-eight hundred baseline, so they continue for two more months and reach forty-two hundred saved.

At that point they shift to living on last month's income by using that forty-two hundred saved to fund all of next month's baseline expenses, while that month's actual income of fifty-five hundred goes into savings untouched. The following month they use the fifty-five hundred to fund baseline of thirty-eight hundred plus taxes of eleven hundred plus some discretionary spending, while that month's actual income again goes into savings. They're now living one month ahead and the mental shift is huge because they're never worried about whether income will arrive in time to cover expenses.

The envelope method adapted for digital banking means creating multiple categories or "envelopes" where we allocate money mentally or through software features, even though it all sits in the same account. Traditional envelope budgeting used physical cash divided into physical envelopes for different expense categories, but most of our spending happens digitally now so we need a digital version that creates the same psychological boundaries without requiring cash.

Digital tools that support envelope budgeting include YNAB which is built entirely around this concept, allowing us to create categories and assign dollars to them as income arrives, then tracking spending against those assignments to make sure we don't overspend any category. Other options like EveryDollar or Goodbudget work similarly, creating virtual envelopes we fund with each paycheck or income deposit, then tracking as we spend from each envelope.

The variable income version of envelope budgeting means our envelope amounts change month to month based on actual income, unlike traditional envelope budgeting where the same amount goes in each envelope every time. When we earn six thousand we might put four hundred in the groceries envelope and three hundred in the entertainment envelope, but when we earn four thousand we might put three hundred in groceries and one hundred in entertainment, scaling the envelopes to match available money while prioritizing the important ones.

Some categories need to be flexible because the amount we need to spend varies based on circumstances, while other categories should stay fixed because the expense doesn't change with our mood or situation. Groceries is somewhat flexible because we can choose cheaper options when money is tight, but we can't drop it to zero so it needs a minimum allocation even in bad months. Entertainment is fully flexible because we can skip it entirely if needed. Rent is fixed because it doesn't matter what we want to spend, we owe what we owe.

Choosing which budgeting method fits our situation and personality matters more than choosing the "best" method because they all work if we actually use them, and none of them work if they're too complicated or annoying for us to maintain. The person who loves spreadsheets and detailed tracking might do great with zero-sum budgeting in a custom spreadsheet, while the person who finds that overwhelming might need YNAB or a simpler app that does most of the thinking for them.

The freelancer with relatively stable income might do fine with percentage-based budgeting like the modified 50/30/20 rule, while the freelancer with wild income swings needs priority-based budgeting that handles months when income is thirty percent of average without falling apart. Someone who's generally organized and disciplined might succeed with any method, while someone who struggles with follow-through needs the simplest possible system with the least friction.

Real freelancers using different methods show how this plays out in practice. The writer using zero-sum budgeting allocates every dollar of the fifty-two hundred they earned this month, funding baseline of thirty-four hundred, taxes of thirteen hundred, buffer of three hundred, and emergency fund of two hundred, ending at exactly zero unallocated. The designer using priority hierarchy funds baseline of thirty-eight hundred first from income of forty-five hundred, then taxes of nine hundred, then buffer of five hundred, then business growth of two hundred, then has nothing left for discretionary so that's zero this month.

The developer living on last month's income budgets February spending using January's income of sixty-eight hundred, allocating forty-two hundred to baseline, seventeen hundred to taxes, nine hundred to discretionary, and letting February's actual income of fifty-four hundred sit untouched ready to fund March. The consultant using modified percentages on income of seventy-five hundred allocates thirty-seven fifty to business plus salary, twenty-two fifty to growth and development, and fifteen hundred to taxes and savings, though they're running short on taxes and will need to adjust.

Hybrid approaches work better than pure adherence to any single method because real life is messier than budgeting theory, and we might use zero-sum budgeting for regular monthly planning but switch to strict priority hierarchy during unusually tight months, or normally follow percentage guidelines but override them when unexpected expenses show up. The goal is having a system that works most of the time and can handle exceptions when needed, not perfect execution of someone else's ideal method.

The system we choose needs to account for our actual behavior patterns rather than aspirational behavior we hope to have someday, because building a budget around the person we wish we were just sets us up for failure when we act like the person we actually are. If we know we're going to eat out sometimes when stressed, the budget needs to include money for that instead of allocating zero and then feeling guilty when we inevitably spend money on food anyway. If we know we're bad at tracking every transaction, we need a method that doesn't require perfect tracking instead of choosing one that does and then failing.

Starting with the simplest version of whichever method appeals to us makes way more sense than trying to build the perfect complex system right away, because simple systems we actually use beat perfect systems we abandon after two weeks. We can always add complexity later if we find we need it, but starting complex almost guarantees we'll give up when it gets overwhelming.

The test of whether our budgeting method works is whether we're still using it three months from now and whether it's actually helping us make better financial decisions, not whether it perfectly matches some expert's recommendation or uses the most sophisticated tools. A simple spreadsheet we update weekly beats expensive software we never open, and a rough priority system we follow beats detailed zero-sum budgeting we abandon because it's too much work.

The Complete Tax Game

Self-employment tax hits us like a brick wall the first time we see it calculated because nobody warned us that we're paying both sides of Social Security and Medicare, the employee half we'd pay anyway plus the employer half that was invisible when someone else was cutting our paycheck. The total comes to 15.3% of our net self-employment income right off the top before we even start thinking about federal or state income taxes, and when we add everything together we're looking at sending somewhere between twenty-five and forty percent of our income to various tax authorities depending on how much we make and where we live.

The 15.3% breaks down into two pieces that work slightly differently, with Social Security taking 12.4% of our net income up to a cap that adjusts annually and currently sits at $176,100 for 2025, meaning once our income exceeds that amount we stop paying Social Security tax on anything above it. Medicare takes 2.9% with no income cap at all, so we're paying that percentage on every dollar we earn no matter how high our income goes, plus an additional 0.9% Medicare tax kicks in once we hit $200,000 for single filers or $250,000 for married filing jointly, bringing the Medicare portion to 3.8% on income above those thresholds.

Employees pay half of this while their employer pays the other half, so they see 7.65% coming out of their paycheck for Social Security and Medicare combined, but we're paying the full 15.3% ourselves because we are both the employee and the employer when we're self-employed. This isn't doubling our taxes compared to employment, it's just making visible the full cost that was always there but partially hidden when someone else handled the employer portion, though it definitely feels like doubling when we're used to only seeing the employee half deducted.

Federal income tax on top of self-employment tax depends on our total income and filing status, running from ten percent on the first chunk of income up to thirty-seven percent on income above a pretty high threshold most freelancers never reach. The brackets for 2025 put us at ten percent on roughly the first eleven thousand we make, twelve percent on income from eleven thousand to forty-seven thousand, twenty-two percent from forty-seven thousand to one hundred six thousand, and higher percentages beyond that for those earning more.

State income tax varies wildly depending where we live, with some states like Texas and Florida having zero income tax while others like California hit us for another nine percent or more on top of everything else. We need to know our specific state's tax rate to calculate accurately, but for planning purposes assuming somewhere between zero and eight percent for most states gets us close enough, and we can adjust once we know the exact number.

Adding all these together shows why the standard advice to set aside thirty percent of every payment makes sense even though it sounds excessive at first. Someone in the twenty-two percent federal bracket paying 15.3% self-employment tax and five percent state tax is looking at total tax burden over forty percent, though some of that comes back through deductions and the self-employment tax deduction that reduces our taxable income, bringing the effective rate down to something closer to thirty to thirty-five percent for most freelancers earning between fifty and one hundred thousand annually.

The calculation gets simpler when we just set aside thirty percent automatically and adjust later if it turns out we need more or less, because the goal isn't precision in predicting our exact tax bill, it's making sure we have enough money saved when quarterly payments come due and annual filing happens. Better to save too much and get a pleasant surprise at tax time than save too little and scramble to find thousands we don't have, especially since money we oversaved for taxes can be redirected to emergency fund or buffer once we know we don't need it for the IRS.

Setting up the automatic transfer to tax savings means linking our business account to a separate savings account designated for taxes and nothing else, then either manually transferring thirty percent every time a payment hits or using automation features if our bank offers them to move the money without us thinking about it. The manual approach takes discipline but gives us more control, while the automatic approach removes the temptation to skip transfers when money feels tight.

Real example with actual numbers shows a freelancer receiving a $4,200 client payment, immediately transferring $1,260 to tax savings at exactly thirty percent, leaving $2,940 in the business account available for salary and expenses. Another payment of $1,800 triggers a transfer of $540 to tax savings, another payment of $3,500 moves $1,050 to taxes, and by the end of the month they've received total payments of $12,400 and moved $3,720 to tax savings, leaving $8,680 for everything else.

That freelancer's actual tax obligation might be slightly different than the thirty percent they saved, but they're in the right ballpark and won't face any nasty surprises when quarterly payments come due. If their actual taxes turn out to be twenty-eight percent they'll have saved a bit too much, which they can adjust going forward or just leave as extra buffer in the tax account. If their taxes are thirty-two percent they'll be slightly short but not catastrophically so, and they can adjust to saving thirty-two or thirty-three percent going forward.

Quarterly estimated tax payments confuse a lot of freelancers because we're used to annual tax filing and the idea of sending money to the IRS four times a year feels weird and complicated even though it's actually simpler than trying to save up a huge lump sum to pay once annually. The IRS wants us paying taxes roughly as we earn the income, same as employees have taxes withheld from every paycheck, and quarterly payments are how we accomplish that without having an employer doing withholding for us.

The requirement to pay quarterly kicks in when we expect to owe at least a thousand dollars in tax for the year after accounting for any withholding or credits, which covers basically every freelancer making more than minimal income. The deadlines fall roughly every three months but don't line up perfectly with calendar quarters, hitting April 15th for income earned January through March, June 15th for April through May, September 15th for June through August, and January 15th of the following year for September through December, which means the second quarter is only two months and the fourth quarter is four months but we're still making four equal payments.

Calculating how much to send each quarter starts with estimating our total annual net self-employment income by looking at what we've earned so far and projecting forward based on our typical patterns, though this gets easier after our first year when we have actual history to reference. Net income means gross income minus business expenses, so if we earned $75,000 in payments but spent $15,000 on business expenses, our net is $60,000 and that's what we calculate taxes on.

Form 1040-ES walks through the calculation with worksheets that feel intimidating the first time through but become routine once we've done it a few times, asking us to estimate our income, calculate self-employment tax and income tax, subtract any credits we qualify for, and divide the result by four to get our quarterly payment amount. The form includes payment vouchers we can mail with a check if we're doing it old school, though most people pay electronically now through IRS Direct Pay or the Electronic Federal Tax Payment System.

The safe harbor rule protects us from underpayment penalties even if our estimates turn out wrong, as long as we meet one of two tests by paying either ninety percent of what we'll actually owe for the current year or one hundred percent of what we owed last year, whichever is smaller. For high earners who made over $150,000 adjusted gross income last year, the safe harbor threshold rises to one hundred ten percent of last year's tax, which is higher but still achievable.

Using last year's tax as our safe harbor target makes quarterly calculations way easier because we know exactly what we owed last year, we divide that by four, and we send that amount each quarter regardless of how this year is actually going. If we owed $12,000 total tax last year we send $3,000 per quarter this year and we're protected from penalties no matter what happens with our actual income, though if we earn significantly more this year we'll owe the difference at filing time.

The alternative is calculating quarterly based on actual income each quarter, which gives us a more accurate running total but requires more work and creates risk if we underestimate. Some freelancers prefer this method because it means their quarterly payments reflect their actual situation and they're less likely to owe a big chunk at filing time, while others prefer the simplicity of just using last year's number and adjusting once when filing rather than four times throughout the year.

Payment methods include the IRS Direct Pay system which pulls money directly from our bank account for free, the Electronic Federal Tax Payment System that requires setting up an account but offers more features, paying through our IRS online account if we've set one up, using a credit or debit card through approved payment processors though they charge fees of around two percent, or mailing a check though that option is being phased out and was supposed to end in late 2025.

Most freelancers find Direct Pay easiest because there's no setup required beyond having our Social Security number and bank account information handy, the transaction processes immediately so we know it went through, and there's zero fees or charges. The system saves our bank information for future payments if we want, making subsequent quarterly payments even faster, and we get immediate confirmation that the IRS received our payment.

Missing a quarterly payment or underpaying triggers penalty and interest charges from the IRS calculated based on how much we should have paid and how long we went without paying it, though the penalty isn't huge if we're only slightly off or only miss one quarter. The IRS calculates underpayment penalty at whatever their current interest rate is, typically around seven or eight percent annually, applied to the amount we should have paid for the period we didn't pay it, which works out to maybe fifty to a hundred dollars on a thousand dollar shortfall over a few months.

We can catch up on missed quarters by paying extra in the next quarter, though we'll still owe the penalty on the missed payment so better to just pay on time in the first place. The penalty isn't the end of the world if life gets chaotic and we miss one deadline, but chronically missing quarters or seriously underpaying creates a pattern the IRS notices and potentially triggers an audit or collection action, so we want to stay current even if our estimates aren't perfect.

State quarterly payments work similarly for states that have income tax, with their own deadlines that usually but don't always match the federal deadlines and their own calculation worksheets that usually but don't always work the same as federal. We need to check our specific state's tax authority website to see what they require, though most states make it pretty straightforward once we know where to look.

Business expense deductions reduce our net income which reduces our taxes, which is why tracking business expenses matters beyond just knowing where money went. Every dollar we spend on legitimate business expenses is a dollar we don't pay taxes on, so a five hundred dollar laptop purchase for work saves us roughly one hundred fifty in taxes assuming we're in the thirty percent effective tax bracket, making the laptop's actual cost to us three hundred fifty instead of five hundred.

The home office deduction lets us write off part of our housing costs if we have a dedicated space used regularly and exclusively for business, calculated either by measuring the square footage of our office as a percentage of our home's total square footage, or using the simplified method that allows five dollars per square foot up to three hundred square feet. The regular method requires tracking actual expenses like rent, utilities, insurance, and maintenance then deducting our percentage, while the simplified method just multiplies our office square footage by five dollars and we're done.

Qualifying for the home office deduction requires genuine exclusive use of the space, meaning if our desk is in the living room where we also watch TV and hang out, it doesn't count, but if we have a spare bedroom that's set up as an office and we don't use it for anything else, that qualifies. The IRS takes this seriously and will disallow the deduction if they audit us and find we're not actually using the space exclusively for business.

Equipment and software we buy for business gets deducted either all at once in the year we buy it if we're using Section 179 expensing for items under a pretty high dollar threshold, or depreciated over several years if we're using standard depreciation rules for more expensive items. Most freelancers use Section 179 because it's simpler and gets us the full deduction immediately rather than spreading it across multiple years, and the threshold for 2025 is over a million dollars so we'd need to be buying extremely expensive equipment to exceed it.

Internet and phone bills are partially deductible based on the percentage we use them for business versus personal use, so if we use our phone fifty percent for business we deduct fifty percent of the bill. We're supposed to have some reasonable method for determining this percentage, like tracking actual calls for a representative period, rather than just guessing, though many freelancers do in fact guess and hope they don't get audited.

Professional development expenses like courses, books, conferences, and subscriptions to industry publications are fully deductible as long as they're genuinely related to our current business and not training us for a completely new field. The web developer taking an advanced JavaScript course can deduct it, but the web developer taking a course on becoming a real estate agent probably can't because that's training for a different business entirely.

Marketing and advertising costs are fully deductible including website hosting, domain registration, business cards, online ads, social media promotion, and anything else we spend trying to attract clients. The designer paying for a premium portfolio site and running Instagram ads can deduct both, the writer paying for a professional website redesign can deduct that, the consultant paying for LinkedIn Premium to get better lead gen features can deduct that.

Business insurance including professional liability, general liability, errors and omissions, and whatever other coverage we carry gets deducted in full as a business expense. Health insurance premiums get deducted differently, going on our personal tax return as an adjustment to income rather than as a business expense, but they're still deductible which is what matters.

Professional fees we pay to accountants, bookkeepers, lawyers, or other professionals who help us run the business are fully deductible, which means the five hundred we pay our accountant to prepare our tax return saves us about one hundred fifty in taxes, making the accountant's net cost three hundred fifty. This is why hiring professional help often pays for itself through better deductions and avoided mistakes.

Office supplies, shipping costs, bank fees, merchant processing fees, contract labor we pay to other freelancers, travel expenses for business trips with specific documentation requirements, and fifty percent of business meal costs all count as deductible expenses that reduce our taxable income. The key is having receipts or records proving we actually spent the money and it was actually for business rather than personal use.

Record keeping for all these deductions means saving receipts either physically or digitally, noting what each expense was for in case we forget later, categorizing everything in our accounting software so we can pull reports at tax time, and keeping everything organized enough that we could find documentation if the IRS ever questions something. The standard recommendation is keeping tax records for at least three years after filing, though seven years is safer for anything the IRS might consider suspicious.

Monthly expense review keeps our deductions organized without requiring a huge scramble at year end, and takes maybe thirty minutes to go through the month's transactions, make sure everything's categorized correctly, upload receipts to our storage system, and spot any weird charges that might be errors or fraud. Building this habit throughout the year beats trying to reconstruct twelve months of expenses in March while stressed about the filing deadline.

The tax savings account balance should grow steadily throughout the year as we add thirty percent of each payment, then drop sharply when we make quarterly payments, then grow again, creating a sawtooth pattern that levels out around having enough saved for the next quarter plus a buffer for annual filing. By the end of the year we should have saved enough to cover both our fourth quarter payment and our annual filing with maybe a small surplus or small shortfall depending on how accurate our thirty percent estimate was.

Real example shows tax savings account starting the year at zero, growing to $4,500 by March when we pay first quarter of $3,800, dropping to $700, growing to $5,200 by June when we pay second quarter of $3,800, dropping to $1,400, growing to $5,800 by September when we pay third quarter of $3,800, dropping to $2,000, growing to $6,400 by December, paying fourth quarter of $3,800 in January, dropping to $2,600, then using that remaining amount toward annual filing in April.

That pattern means we're always ahead of our quarterly obligations and never scrambling to find tax money, which is exactly the point of automatic transfers throughout the year. Some months we're adding more to tax savings than others based on income variability, but the general trend is upward between payment dates and we're never wondering how we'll make the next quarterly payment.

Adjusting the thirty percent up or down happens after our first year when we can see our actual effective tax rate and compare it to what we saved, making the second year more accurate than the first just through having real data instead of estimates. If we saved thirty percent but only owed twenty-six percent, we can drop to twenty-seven percent going forward and have more cash available monthly. If we saved thirty percent but owed thirty-four percent, we need to increase to thirty-five percent and accept that less cash is available monthly but we won't face a surprise bill.

The goal isn't perfection in predicting our exact tax obligation, it's having enough saved that we're never stressed about quarterly payments or annual filing, and finding ourselves with a small refund or small balance due at year end rather than a huge swing either direction. Once we've got the system running smoothly, taxes become routine rather than terrifying, just another business expense we plan for like rent or software subscriptions.

Building Our Safety Net

The difference between needing six months of emergency savings as an employee versus twelve months as a freelancer comes down to what happens when income stops, because employees can collect unemployment benefits while job hunting and have some predictable timeline for when new income might start, while freelancers get absolutely nothing from the government and face a completely unpredictable timeline for replacing lost income. We can't file for unemployment when a major client cancels their retainer or projects dry up, we just have to figure it out ourselves using whatever resources we've managed to save, which is why the standard three to six month advice doesn't cut it for our situation.

Employees who lose their job can typically expect to find new employment within three to six months if they're actively looking and have marketable skills, and during that time they're collecting unemployment checks that cover at least part of their previous income. Freelancers who lose a major client or hit a dry spell might spend two months landing new clients, another month completing the first projects, and another month or two waiting for those invoices to actually get paid, easily hitting six months from problem to resolution even if everything goes relatively smoothly.

The timeline extends further when we factor in that building back to our previous income level might take longer than just replacing a single lost client, because we probably need multiple new clients to replace one big one, and finding multiple good clients simultaneously is harder than finding one. The freelancer who was earning six thousand monthly from three clients averaging two thousand each might replace a lost client within a month, but the freelancer who was earning six thousand monthly from one client at six thousand faces a much longer rebuild time because finding another six thousand dollar client is significantly harder than finding a two thousand dollar one.

Industry downturns hit freelancers harder than employees because when companies start cutting budgets, freelancers and contractors are usually the first to go since we're considered variable costs rather than fixed employees, which means during recessions or sector-specific slowdowns we're dealing with widespread client loss rather than just individual relationship issues. The designer working primarily with tech startups during a tech downturn might see half their client base disappear simultaneously, requiring a complete pivot to different industries while income drops to nearly nothing.

Illness or injury that prevents us from working creates immediate income stoppage with no disability insurance unless we specifically bought a policy ourselves, which most freelancers haven't because it's expensive and we're optimistically assuming we'll stay healthy. Breaking an arm might not stop an employee's income since they're still getting paid even if they're not productive, but it completely stops a freelance graphic designer's income since they literally cannot work and therefore cannot bill clients.

Building an emergency fund that actually protects against these scenarios means having six to twelve months of our baseline essential expenses saved in an accessible account where we can get the money immediately if needed without penalties or waiting periods. Not six to twelve months of our total current spending including all discretionary expenses, but six to twelve months of what we absolutely must spend to maintain housing, utilities, food, insurance, transportation, and minimum debt payments.

The calculation starts with our baseline number from chapter one, which should be the truly essential expenses we cannot skip without creating immediate crisis, multiplied by six for the minimum emergency fund or by twelve for the more secure version. A freelancer with thirty-five hundred in baseline essential expenses needs twenty-one thousand for six months or forty-two thousand for twelve months, which sounds like an impossible amount until we remember this is a multi-year goal we're building toward gradually, not something we need to accomplish next month.

Separating the buffer fund from the emergency fund keeps these two different financial tools serving their different purposes without getting confused, because buffer exists to smooth monthly income variations and gets used regularly while emergency fund exists to handle genuine emergencies and shouldn't get touched except in serious situations. The buffer lives in our business account holding two to three months of salary and handling the normal ups and downs of freelance income, while emergency fund lives in a separate personal savings account holding six to twelve months of baseline expenses and only getting tapped when something truly bad happens.

Using emergency fund for non-emergencies is how we end up with no emergency fund when an actual emergency hits, because if we're pulling from it every time we have a slow month or want to buy something we can't quite afford, it never grows to the point where it actually protects us. The slow month situation is what buffer handles, and the want-to-buy-something situation is what our discretionary budget handles, leaving emergency fund exclusively for the job-loss or major-illness or other serious crisis scenarios it was built for.

Real emergencies that justify using the emergency fund include losing a major client who represented significant portion of our income without warning, industry-wide downturn that kills demand for our services across the board, serious illness or injury that prevents us from working for an extended period, family emergency requiring us to stop working to provide care, major life disruption like divorce or death of spouse, and other genuinely crisis-level situations where our normal income and buffer aren't sufficient to handle the problem.

Not-actually-emergencies that we're tempted to use emergency fund for but shouldn't include slow months within our normal range of income variability because that's what buffer handles, wanting to buy new equipment or upgrade our setup when what we have still works fine, taking a vacation we can't afford from our current discretionary budget, covering overspending in other categories because we didn't stick to our budget, and basically anything that could have been planned for or avoided with better regular budgeting.

The percentage method for building emergency fund means setting aside a specific percentage of every payment or every month's income toward emergency savings, typically somewhere between ten and twenty percent depending on how much margin we have after covering baseline, taxes, and buffer. This scales automatically with income so we're saving more during good months and less during slow months, which matches our variable income reality better than trying to save a fixed dollar amount regardless of how much we earned.

Real example shows a freelancer saving fifteen percent of monthly income toward emergency fund, which comes out to nine hundred when they earn six thousand, six hundred seventy-five when they earn forty-five hundred, and twelve hundred when they earn eight thousand. Over a year with mixed income averaging sixty-three hundred monthly, they save roughly eleven thousand toward emergency fund, getting halfway to their six-month goal of twenty-one thousand in the first year.

The fixed amount method means deciding we'll save a specific dollar amount every month toward emergency fund regardless of income, which works better when we have relatively stable income or when we're committed enough to cut other spending during slow months to maintain the savings rate. This approach builds emergency fund on a more predictable timeline since we know exactly how much we're adding each month, but requires more discipline when income is low because we're still moving that fixed amount to savings even when it hurts.

Real example shows a freelancer committing to save five hundred monthly toward emergency fund no matter what, which means during a forty-five hundred income month they're saving eleven percent, during a six thousand income month they're saving eight percent, and during an eight thousand income month they're saving just over six percent. The declining percentage as income rises feels backward, but the point is consistency in building the fund rather than perfectly proportional saving, and over twelve months they'll add exactly six thousand to emergency fund regardless of income swings.

The surplus method saves whatever's left after covering all other obligations, which is the least predictable approach but works for freelancers who have highly variable income and can't commit to either a percentage or a fixed amount. During great months when income far exceeds expenses this method can add substantial amounts to emergency fund, but during tight months nothing gets saved, making progress irregular and potentially slow.

Real example shows a freelancer earning seven thousand in January with baseline of thirty-eight hundred and taxes of two thousand one hundred, leaving one thousand one hundred after also funding some buffer and discretionary spending, all of which goes to emergency fund. February income of forty-five hundred barely covers baseline and taxes with nothing left over, so zero goes to emergency fund. March income of six thousand five hundred leaves nine hundred after everything else, going to emergency fund. The irregular deposits mean slower progress than the other methods but require less discipline and work with any income pattern.

Combining all three methods creates the most robust approach where we have a minimum percentage we always save like ten percent, try to hit a fixed amount like four hundred monthly when possible, and anything above that target during surplus months goes to emergency fund as well. This gives us consistent baseline progress through the percentage requirement, additional progress through the fixed amount goal, and accelerated progress through surplus deposits, building emergency fund as fast as our income and discipline allow.

Automating the emergency fund transfers makes them happen without requiring active decision making each time we get paid, which matters because in the moment we'll always be able to think of better uses for that money than putting it in savings where we can't touch it. Setting up automatic transfers of our percentage or fixed amount on the same schedule we pay ourselves means the money disappears into emergency fund before we're tempted to spend it on something else.

The best place to keep emergency fund money balances accessibility with growth, because we need to be able to get the money quickly if genuine emergency hits but we also want it earning at least some interest rather than sitting completely idle. High yield savings accounts paying anywhere from two to five percent annual interest depending on current rates work well because we can access the money same-day or next-day without penalties, it's FDIC insured up to two hundred fifty thousand so there's no risk of loss, and it's growing slowly while sitting there waiting to be needed.

Money market accounts work similarly to high yield savings with comparable interest rates and similar accessibility, sometimes offering check-writing features if we want that convenience though we probably don't need it for emergency fund. The main difference is money markets might have higher minimum balance requirements, which matters when we're just starting to build the fund but becomes irrelevant once we've got substantial savings.

What we should avoid keeping emergency fund in includes regular checking accounts that pay nearly zero interest and are too easy to access for non-emergencies, stock market investments that could drop in value right when we need the money most, crypto or other highly volatile assets that might be worth half as much next month as they are today, CDs or other time-locked accounts that charge penalties for early withdrawal, and physical cash that earns nothing and creates security risk.

The psychological barrier that makes building emergency fund so hard is that we're setting aside thousands of dollars for something we hope never happens, which feels wasteful compared to spending that money on things we can enjoy now or investing it for potential growth. We're essentially buying insurance in the form of savings, and like all insurance it feels like a waste until the day we need it, at which point we're incredibly grateful it exists.

Reframing emergency fund as buying peace of mind rather than wasting money helps with the psychological resistance, because what we're actually purchasing with those monthly deposits is the ability to sleep at night without worrying that one bad month could destroy our entire financial life. The freelancer with no emergency fund lives with constant background anxiety about what happens if clients disappear or they get sick, while the freelancer with twelve months saved can weather almost anything without panic.

The timeline for building from zero to six months of expenses saved depends entirely on our income level and how much margin we have after covering baseline and taxes, but most freelancers with decent income should be able to hit six months within eighteen to twenty-four months if they're making it a priority. Twelve months of expenses saved might take three to four years starting from zero, which sounds like forever but is still achievable with consistent effort.

Real timeline for a freelancer starting with zero emergency fund and baseline of thirty-two hundred shows them saving four hundred monthly on average through a combination of ten percent of income plus occasional surplus deposits. After six months they have twenty-four hundred saved, less than one month of baseline. After twelve months they have forty-eight hundred, one and a half months of baseline. After eighteen months they have seventy-two hundred, over two months of baseline. After twenty-four months they have ninety-six hundred, exactly three months of baseline or halfway to their six-month goal.

That progression feels painfully slow when we're in the middle of it, but comparing where we are after two years to where we started shows massive improvement in financial security. The freelancer with ninety-six hundred saved can handle a two-month dry spell without crisis, can deal with unexpected car repairs or medical bills without derailing their finances, and has room to be selective about which clients to work with because they're not desperate for every dollar.

Continuing the same four hundred monthly savings brings them to one hundred ninety-two hundred after four years, exactly six months of baseline saved, reaching the minimum emergency fund goal we set. Getting to twelve months takes another four years of consistent saving if income and savings rate stay the same, which might accelerate if income grows or we decide to prioritize emergency fund more heavily by increasing the percentage we save.

Rebuilding the emergency fund after we've had to use it for actual emergency is critical because once we've established that financial security we don't want to go back to living without it, which means treating the rebuild as urgent priority even though the immediate crisis has passed. The freelancer who had to use six thousand from emergency fund to cover expenses during a three-month client loss needs to rebuild that six thousand before considering the emergency fund fully restored, ideally doubling their normal savings rate until the fund is back to previous levels.

Starting with a one-month goal instead of immediately shooting for six or twelve months makes the whole project feel achievable rather than impossibly overwhelming, because saving thirty-five hundred or four thousand feels doable within a few months while saving twenty-five or forty thousand feels impossible. Once we hit one month saved we get psychological momentum from seeing the progress and can aim for two months, then three, building gradually rather than getting discouraged and giving up.

Celebrating milestones along the way helps maintain motivation through what is genuinely a multi-year project requiring sustained discipline, so we might treat ourselves to something small but meaningful when we hit each month of expenses saved, or take a moment to acknowledge we've achieved something most freelancers never manage. Hitting three months saved is worth recognizing even though we're not done yet, because three months of security is infinitely better than zero months of security and represents real financial progress.

The emergency fund working together with our buffer fund creates a two-layer protection system where buffer handles normal variability and emergency fund handles actual crisis, which means we're protected against both routine slow months and genuinely catastrophic situations. Most financial stress freelancers experience comes from routine variability that buffer would handle, and the rare but devastating stress comes from actual emergencies that emergency fund covers, so having both in place eliminates almost all the financial anxiety that makes freelancing feel so unstable.

Some freelancers resist building emergency fund because they want to invest money for growth rather than letting it sit in savings earning minimal interest, arguing they could be making eight or ten percent returns in the stock market instead of three or four percent in a high yield savings account. This logic ignores the fact that emergency fund serves a completely different purpose than investments, providing insurance and stability rather than growth, and trying to use investments for emergency money means we might have to sell at a loss during a market downturn right when we need the cash most.

The right sequence is building emergency fund first until we have at least six months saved, then starting to invest additional savings for growth, rather than investing everything and hoping we never need emergency money. Once emergency fund is solid we can be more aggressive with any savings beyond that amount, but the foundation needs to be stable before we start taking investment risk.

Accessing emergency fund when we actually need it should be simple and fast since we kept it in a high yield savings account rather than anywhere with withdrawal restrictions, but we still want to think carefully before pulling that money out to make sure what we're facing is genuinely an emergency and not just a situation we could handle differently. The slow month that feels scary but is actually within our normal income range should be covered by buffer not emergency fund, even though in the moment both feel like emergencies.

Once we've determined we really do need emergency money, transferring it from savings to checking to cover expenses is usually just a few clicks in our bank's app or website, with the money available same day or next day depending on the bank. We take what we actually need rather than withdrawing more just because it's there, and we note how much we withdrew so we know what we need to rebuild once the crisis passes.

The emergency fund reaching our target level of six or twelve months doesn't mean we stop saving, it means we can redirect that saving toward other goals like retirement investing, business growth, or whatever else matters to us financially. But we do want to maintain the emergency fund at its target level rather than letting it dwindle because we stopped paying attention, which means if we use some of it we rebuild it before redirecting savings elsewhere.

Pricing to Stop the Struggle

Charging too little creates a situation where we're working constantly but never getting ahead financially, always busy with projects that pay just enough to cover immediate expenses but leave nothing for savings or buffer building, and this trap is way more common among freelancers than charging too much because we're terrified of losing clients by asking for what our work is actually worth. The designer billing thirty dollars an hour when their work is worth seventy-five is working more than twice as hard as necessary to earn the same total income, and that extra effort compounds into burnout and resentment even though they're the one who set the rate in the first place.

Underpricing usually comes from imposter syndrome making us feel like we're not actually qualified to charge what experienced people in our field charge, combined with seeing cheaper competitors and assuming we need to match their rates to get work, but both of these assumptions fall apart when we examine them closely. The competitor charging half what everyone else charges is either brand new and doesn't know better yet, or isn't actually getting much work at that rate because clients who can afford to pay more choose more expensive options assuming higher price means higher quality.

The psychology of pricing is that clients often use price as a signal for quality when they can't easily evaluate the work itself before buying, which means our cheap rates might actually be costing us clients who would happily pay more but assume we're not very good because we're charging so little. The business owner looking for a designer to handle an important project sees quotes ranging from twenty-five to one hundred fifty per hour and often picks someone in the middle to upper range rather than the cheapest option, because they're worried the cheap person will do cheap work and create more problems than they solve.

Breaking out of underpricing requires first understanding what we should actually be charging based on our skill level, experience, and market rates, then raising our rates for new clients immediately while gradually transitioning existing clients to higher rates over some reasonable period. We don't need to jump from thirty to seventy-five overnight for everyone, but we should stop accepting new work at rates that don't reflect our actual value, and we should be actively working toward getting all our clients paying fair rates within six months to a year.

Hourly pricing creates a straightforward relationship where we track time spent and multiply by our rate, making it easy to calculate what we'll earn and easy for clients to understand what they'll pay, but it also caps our income based on available hours and penalizes us for getting faster and more efficient at our work. The developer who can now build a feature in four hours that used to take eight is earning half as much for the same deliverable even though their skill improvement should make them more valuable not less, and this backwards incentive is why experienced freelancers tend to move away from hourly billing.

The efficiency penalty hits hardest when we're billing by the hour and learning or improving at our craft, because all that improvement directly reduces our income unless we raise rates constantly to compensate. A designer charging fifty per hour who takes ten hours to complete a logo in their first year is earning five hundred per logo, but two years later when they've gotten good enough to do the same quality work in three hours, they're earning one hundred fifty per logo unless they've raised their rate to something like eighty or ninety per hour.

Clients sometimes get uncomfortable with hourly billing because they're worried about the final cost spinning out of control if the project takes longer than estimated, which creates pressure on us to lowball our estimates to win the work, then we end up eating hours when the project inevitably takes longer than our optimistic estimate. The client who approved ten hours at seventy-five dollars isn't going to be happy when we bill them for eighteen hours, even if those eighteen hours were genuinely necessary, so we either absorb the extra eight hours and work for free or damage the relationship by billing the real amount.

Project-based pricing flips the incentive structure so we're rewarded for efficiency rather than penalized, charging a fixed amount for a defined deliverable regardless of how long it takes us to complete it. The same logo project might be priced at twelve hundred dollars whether it takes us three hours or twelve hours, which means getting faster and better at our work directly increases our effective hourly rate rather than decreasing it.

The value to the client is getting predictable pricing they can budget for without worrying about hour tracking or cost overruns, and the value to us is being able to improve our efficiency without cutting our own income. The client knows they're paying twelve hundred for a professional logo regardless of the details, and we know we're earning twelve hundred for the work regardless of whether we nail it on the first try or need several rounds of revisions.

Setting project prices requires estimating how long something will take us at our current skill level, multiplying that by what we'd charge hourly, then adding a buffer for the inevitable revisions and scope creep that happen on most projects. The designer who thinks a logo will take five hours at seventy-five per hour might quote eight hundred instead of three seventy-five, building in three extra hours worth of rate to cover the revisions that always happen, which still ends up cheaper for the client than if the project actually took eight hours billed hourly.

Market research helps calibrate our project pricing by showing us what others charge for similar work, though we need to be careful about comparing ourselves to either the absolute cheapest competitors who are underpricing or the most expensive boutique firms who have brand recognition and premium positioning we don't have. Looking at the middle range of what established but not famous freelancers charge gives us a realistic target for where our prices should land.

Value-based pricing takes project pricing further by considering what the deliverable is worth to the client rather than just what it costs us in time to produce, charging based on the impact or benefit the client receives. The consultant helping a business implement a process change that saves them fifty thousand annually might charge five or ten thousand for that consulting work even if it only takes twenty hours, because the value delivered is massive compared to the time invested.

This approach works best when we can clearly identify and articulate the value our work creates, which is easier in some fields than others. The copywriter who writes sales page copy that increases conversion rates by two percent on a product doing a million in annual sales is creating twenty thousand in additional revenue, making it reasonable to charge two or three thousand for the copy work even though it might only take eight to ten hours.

Calculating our real hourly rate starts with figuring out what annual income we need, not want but actually need to cover our expenses and save appropriately, then working backwards to find what hourly rate generates that income based on realistic billable hours. Most freelancers drastically overestimate their billable hours when doing this calculation, assuming they can bill forty hours per week for fifty weeks a year, when reality is more like twenty to twenty-five hours per week actually generate billable work.

The math for someone targeting seventy-five thousand annual income shows we need to divide that by realistic billable hours per year, which might be around a thousand hours if we're working consistently but accounting for time spent on admin, marketing, learning, and all the other non-billable activities required to run a freelance business. Seventy-five thousand divided by a thousand hours is seventy-five per hour, but that's the absolute minimum we need to charge, and we should probably add twenty to thirty percent to that number to build in margin for slower periods and unexpected expenses.

Non-billable time includes everything we do that's necessary for the business but doesn't generate client invoices, like responding to emails, managing our schedule, tracking expenses, doing our bookkeeping, marketing ourselves to potential clients, networking to build relationships, learning new skills to stay current in our field, and dealing with all the administrative overhead that comes with being self-employed. For every hour we bill a client, we're probably spending at least another hour on non-billable activities, which is why we can't assume forty billable hours per week even if we're working full time.

Tracking our actual billable versus non-billable time for a few weeks shows most of us exactly how much of our work week is really billable, and the number is usually shocking because we assumed we were billing way more hours than we actually are. The developer who thought they were billing thirty hours per week might discover they're really only billing eighteen to twenty once they track everything accurately, which explains why their income is lower than expected despite feeling constantly busy.

Building our target rate requires accounting for all the things employees get that we have to pay for ourselves, including the employer portion of Social Security and Medicare taxes we're now paying, health insurance premiums we're covering entirely, retirement savings with no employer match, paid time off that doesn't exist when we're freelance, equipment and software and workspace costs, and the general uncertainty and risk of irregular income. Adding all of this up means our freelance rate needs to be roughly two to three times what an equivalent employee hourly wage would be just to end up with the same take-home income after expenses.

The employee making twenty-five dollars per hour is actually costing their employer closer to thirty-five per hour after payroll taxes, benefits, and overhead, and taking home maybe forty-five thousand annually after taxes. The freelancer trying to match that forty-five thousand take-home needs to charge more like sixty to seventy-five per hour after accounting for self-employment taxes, health insurance, lack of benefits, equipment costs, and non-billable time, which sounds excessive until we do the actual math and realize it barely covers the same lifestyle.

Real example with numbers shows a freelancer calculating they need sixty thousand net income to cover their baseline expenses plus some savings, which means about seventy-eight thousand gross before taxes at thirty percent, which requires billing about ninety-five thousand if we assume some business expenses will be deducted. With a thousand billable hours per year that's ninety-five dollars per hour minimum, and really should be closer to one hundred ten or one hundred twenty to build in margin for variability.

That same freelancer currently charging fifty per hour is earning maybe fifty thousand annually at a thousand billable hours, falling fifteen thousand short of their target gross and twenty-eight thousand short after accounting for the higher taxes they should be paying. They either need to double their hours billed, which is impossible, or double their rate, which feels impossible but is actually the only realistic solution.

Raising rates for existing clients requires planning and communication rather than just sending them a new rate sheet and hoping they don't freak out, because relationships we've built over time are valuable and we don't want to blow them up through clumsy rate increase announcements. The standard approach is giving them at least thirty to sixty days notice, explaining that our rates are increasing to reflect our growing experience and the value we provide, offering to grandfather them at current rates for any projects already in progress, and making it clear we hope to continue working together at the new rates.

Some clients will leave when we raise rates, which hurts but is actually fine because they're the clients who were most focused on getting the cheapest option rather than the best value, and replacing them with clients who pay our new higher rates means we're earning more while working the same amount or less. Losing two clients paying fifty per hour but gaining one client paying a hundred per hour leaves us with the same billable hours but higher income, plus we have more time available to find additional clients at the higher rate.

New client pricing should always be at our current target rate rather than some discounted introductory rate we hope to raise later, because starting low makes it much harder to raise rates down the line and trains the client to expect cheap work from us. If our target rate is ninety dollars per hour, we quote ninety dollars to new prospects even if we're worried they'll say no, because the clients who can afford ninety will say yes and the ones who can't are clients we don't actually want since they won't sustain our business anyway.

The fear that raising rates will mean we get no work at all is almost never founded in reality, because there are clients at every price point and we're just shifting from competing for the bottom-tier clients to competing for middle-tier clients who have bigger budgets and better projects. The designer charging thirty per hour is competing with thousands of designers charging twenty-five to thirty-five, while the designer charging ninety is competing with hundreds charging eighty to one hundred, and that smaller pool of competitors combined with clients who value quality over cheapness usually makes it easier to win work not harder.

Project-based pricing for common deliverables can be standardized so we're not reinventing pricing on every proposal, creating packages like basic website at four thousand, logo design at fifteen hundred, or consultation session at three hundred that we can quote quickly without doing detailed time estimates each time. These package prices should be based on our hourly rate calculation plus buffer for complexity, so if we charge ninety per hour and a basic website typically takes us thirty hours, we might package it at thirty-five hundred rather than twenty-seven hundred to account for the inevitable scope expansion and revision rounds.

Packages work better than pure hourly or pure custom project pricing for many freelancers because clients like the predictability and we like not having to estimate and quote every single variation of work we do, but we need to be willing to say no or charge extra when a client wants something that doesn't fit our standard packages. The website package assumes certain features and complexity, so when a client wants something more involved we need to either quote a custom price or explain which package-plus-additions they actually need.

Retainer pricing provides the holy grail of stable monthly income in exchange for committed availability and a defined scope of work each month, typically billed at a slight discount to our regular rates in exchange for the predictability and reduced overhead of not constantly hunting for new projects. A freelancer charging ninety per hour might offer a monthly retainer of twenty hours for sixteen hundred instead of eighteen hundred, giving the client an eleven percent discount while giving themselves guaranteed income and reduced time spent on sales and client acquisition.

The retainer scope needs to be extremely clear about what twenty hours per month includes and what falls outside that scope, because clients will inevitably try to expand what they expect to get for the retainer rate, and we need to be firm about additional work requiring additional payment. The social media manager on a retainer for twenty hours monthly might include twelve posts, four responses sessions, and one strategy meeting, with any additional posts or meetings being billed separately at their regular project rates.

Weekly or daily rates split the difference between hourly and project pricing, charging a fixed amount for a day or week of availability regardless of exact hours worked during that time, which works well for consulting or ongoing support relationships where clients want consistent access without tracking every hour. A consultant charging ninety per hour might offer a daily rate of six hundred, which looks like a discount if they work less than seven hours but is actually beneficial to both parties because the client gets flexibility and the consultant gets predictable billing without time tracking overhead.

The race to the bottom happens when freelancers compete primarily on price, constantly undercutting each other to win work from clients who only care about paying the least possible amount, which creates a downward spiral where everyone's rates keep dropping until nobody can make a living. Escaping this means refusing to compete on price and instead competing on quality, reliability, expertise, and the specific value we provide that cheap alternatives can't match.

Positioning ourselves as the premium option rather than the budget option requires confidence in our abilities and willingness to turn down work that doesn't pay appropriately, which feels terrifying when we're used to taking whatever we can get, but ultimately leads to a much better client base and much more sustainable income. The freelancer who positions as premium and charges accordingly works with clients who respect their expertise, pay on time, provide clear direction, and don't nickel-and-dime over every detail, while the freelancer competing on price deals with clients who are constantly questioning costs and trying to get more for less.

Real comparison shows a writer charging fifteen cents per word for blog posts, working forty hours per week, producing around eight thousand words weekly, earning about six hundred per week or thirty-one thousand annually while being completely overwhelmed with the volume of writing required. Another writer charging fifty cents per word produces two thousand words weekly in fifteen hours of actual writing time plus five hours of research and client management, earning a thousand per week or fifty-two thousand annually while having time to actually think about their work and maintain quality.

The efficiency of charging more becomes obvious when we realize the higher-priced writer is earning almost twice as much while working half the hours and producing a quarter of the volume, which is only possible because they're charging appropriate rates instead of bargain-basement prices. The lower-priced writer is trapped in a volume game they can't win because there's no way to write fast enough to make poverty wages into decent income.

Raising rates regularly every six to twelve months keeps our pricing aligned with our growing skills and experience rather than staying stuck at whatever we charged when we started, and most clients accept moderate rate increases as normal business practice. A ten to fifteen percent increase annually is reasonable and expected, jumping from seventy-five to eighty-five per hour or from two thousand to twenty-three hundred for a project package, and presenting it matter-of-factly rather than apologetically makes clients much more likely to accept it without complaint.

Some freelancers feel guilty charging more when their costs haven't increased, but our pricing should reflect the value we provide not just our costs, and as we get better at our work we're providing more value in less time which justifies higher rates. The developer who can now solve a problem in two hours that used to take eight is providing the same value to the client faster, which is worth more not less than it was when they were less skilled.

The clients worth keeping are the ones who pay us appropriately and value our work enough to accept reasonable rate increases, while clients who leave over a ten percent rate increase were probably going to be problems eventually anyway. Building a business around clients who respect our value and pay accordingly creates sustainability, while building around clients who only care about getting the cheapest option creates constant stress and eventual burnout.

Keeping Business and Personal Separate

Mixing business money and personal money in the same bank account creates a confusing mess where we can never tell if we're actually profitable or just moving money around, can't track business expenses accurately for tax deductions, and end up making financial decisions based on incomplete information because we don't have a clear picture of either our business health or our personal financial situation. The freelancer with eight thousand in their checking account might think they're doing fine until they remember three thousand of that needs to go to quarterly taxes, two thousand is supposed to cover next month's rent, and only three thousand is actually available to spend, but since it all looks like one number they spend five thousand on a new computer and suddenly can't cover rent.

The confusion multiplies at tax time when we're trying to sort through twelve months of mixed transactions figuring out which purchases were business expenses we can deduct and which were personal spending, wasting hours or days reconstructing our financial history from bank statements and trying to remember whether that Amazon purchase in March was office supplies or personal shopping. The accountant charging us to prepare our taxes ends up charging extra because our records are a disaster, eating into whatever tax savings they might find, and we still end up missing legitimate deductions because we can't prove the expense was actually business-related.

Legal liability issues come up when we're mixing accounts because it makes it harder to demonstrate that we're running a legitimate business rather than just having a hobby, which matters for both tax treatment and potential lawsuit protection if we've set up an LLC or other business entity. The IRS looks at whether we're operating like a real business or like someone who occasionally makes money from their hobby, and businesses have separate finances while hobbies don't, so using one account for everything signals hobby even if we're making substantial income.

Opening a business checking account takes maybe thirty minutes online or an hour if we go to a physical bank branch, requiring our business name or our personal name if we're doing business as ourselves, our Social Security number or EIN if we have one, and answers to some basic questions about what kind of business we run and how much activity we expect. Some banks want to see business registration documents if we have an LLC, but most are fine with sole proprietors opening business accounts using their SSN and just stating they're self-employed.

The features that actually matter in a business account are pretty simple for most freelancers since we're not running complex operations with payroll and merchant processing and all the things bigger businesses need. We need zero or very low monthly fees because paying fifteen or twenty dollars just to have an account is wasteful when free options exist, though we might accept a small fee if the account offers valuable features we'd otherwise pay for separately. We need easy mobile deposit so we can photograph checks if we still get any rather than having to go to a branch, instant or next-day transfers to our personal account without fees or limits, and integration with whatever accounting software we choose so our transactions sync automatically.

Free business checking exists at several online banks and some credit unions, with the tradeoff being no physical branches if we care about that, while traditional banks often charge monthly fees unless we maintain minimum balances that tie up our money. The decision comes down to whether we value physical branch access enough to either pay fees or lock up money in minimum balances, or whether we're fine with everything being digital and keeping our money working rather than sitting idle to avoid fees.

Found offers features specifically designed for freelancers including automatic tax savings where a percentage of each deposit goes to a separate tax pocket, expense categorization that happens as we spend, and integrated invoicing that lets us bill clients directly through the platform. The tradeoff is being locked into their ecosystem and potential issues if they change their features or go out of business, but the convenience of having everything integrated can outweigh the risk of vendor lock-in.

Axos Bank provides free business checking with no monthly fees and no minimum balances, decent interest rates on the balance we do keep, mobile deposit, and standard integration with accounting software, working fine for freelancers who want something straightforward without a lot of extras. Novo works similarly with free business checking, built-in invoicing, and integration with various tools, targeting freelancers and small businesses specifically.

Traditional banks like Chase, Bank of America, or Wells Fargo offer business checking that usually comes with monthly fees unless we maintain substantial minimum balances, but they provide physical branch access if we need to deposit cash or prefer in-person banking for some transactions. The fees typically run fifteen to thirty dollars monthly, which adds up to a couple hundred dollars annually, money that could go toward our emergency fund instead if we don't actually need branch access.

Choosing which bank to use matters less than just getting the account opened and starting to separate our finances, because we can always switch banks later if we find the first one isn't working well, but staying with mixed finances forever creates problems that compound over time. The freelancer who spends three hours researching the perfect bank and never actually opens an account is worse off than the freelancer who picks one that's good enough and opens it this week, even if slightly better options exist.

The personal account can stay wherever we currently bank or we can open a fresh account if we want a clean start, but it needs to be completely separate from the business account with zero business transactions running through it. Every dollar that comes into our personal account should be money we're allowed to spend on our personal life, coming either from our monthly salary transfer or from other personal income sources like a side job or investment returns, never from client payments or business income.

Setting up the transfer system between business and personal accounts means linking them in each bank's online system, usually by providing routing and account numbers and verifying we own both accounts through small test deposits or instant verification through login credentials. Once linked, transfers should be instant or next-day at most, because waiting three to five business days to pay ourselves defeats the purpose of having consistent cash flow.

The actual transfer happens on whatever schedule we set for paying ourselves our monthly salary, either as one lump sum on the first of the month or split into weekly installments if we prefer more frequent smaller deposits. Some banks allow us to set up recurring automatic transfers on a schedule, which removes the need to remember to do it manually each time, while others require us to initiate each transfer ourselves which gives more control but requires more discipline.

All client payments go to the business account period, whether they're paying by check, bank transfer, PayPal, credit card, or any other method, configured so money hits the business account first even if it flows through a payment processor on the way. This keeps our business income completely visible and trackable without having to sort through personal account transactions looking for business deposits, and makes calculating our monthly business income as simple as looking at deposits in the business account.

All business expenses come from the business account using either the business debit card or business checking account number, never mixing in personal payment methods even for small purchases, because the clean separation is what makes the whole system work and mixing even occasionally starts breaking down the boundaries. The fifty dollar software subscription needs to come from business account, the three hundred dollar office chair comes from business account, the twelve dollar domain renewal comes from business account, everything related to the business flows through that one account.

The business credit card question divides freelancers between those who think it's essential and those who think it's unnecessary complication, and both can be right depending on personal spending discipline and whether we can actually pay off the balance monthly. A business credit card used responsibly provides purchase protection, extended warranties on equipment, cash back or rewards on business spending, and another layer of separation between business and personal expenses, but used irresponsibly it's just another way to go into debt and make our financial situation worse.

Opening a business credit card requires decent personal credit since we're personally guaranteeing the debt as a sole proprietor, and works best if we have a real plan to pay the full balance each month rather than carrying balances and paying interest. The rewards can be genuinely valuable if we're spending several thousand monthly on business expenses anyway, potentially earning hundreds in cash back or points annually, but only if we're not paying interest that wipes out the rewards value.

Handling personal emergency needs from business money requires transferring extra to our personal account rather than just spending business money directly on personal stuff, maintaining the clean separation even when we're stressed and tempted to break our own rules. If we need five hundred from business savings to cover an unexpected personal expense, we transfer five hundred from business to personal and then spend it from personal account, keeping the transaction trail clear so we can see exactly when and why we moved money between accounts.

The monthly reconciliation process checks that our business account balance makes sense given income and expenses for the month, our personal account balance makes sense given our salary and spending, and the transfer between them happened as planned. This takes maybe fifteen minutes once we're in the habit, just comparing our accounting software totals to our actual bank balances and making sure nothing weird happened like a double charge or a missed deposit.

Real example shows a freelancer starting the month with forty-two hundred in business account, receiving payments totaling seventy-eight hundred during the month, paying business expenses of twenty-one hundred, transferring salary of thirty-eight hundred to personal account, and ending with forty-one hundred in business account. The seven hundred difference between ending and starting balance represents buffer building from a good month, and the math is completely transparent because everything business-related flowed through one account.

That same freelancer's personal account started the month at eight hundred, received the thirty-eight hundred salary transfer, spent thirty-four hundred on personal expenses including rent and groceries and everything else, and ended at twelve hundred. The four hundred increase in personal account balance represents underspending their salary slightly and having extra for next month or for moving to savings, and again the math is simple because no business transactions muddy the water.

Business entity decisions about whether to stay a sole proprietor or form an LLC or elect S-corporation status affect our taxes and legal liability but don't necessarily change the need for separate accounts, because even sole proprietors benefit from keeping business and personal finances separate for clarity and tax preparation. The choice about business structure should be made based on income level, legal risk in our industry, and tax optimization opportunities rather than just what seems simplest.

Sole proprietorship is the default when we start freelancing, requiring no special registration or paperwork beyond getting business licenses if our city or state requires them, and our business income and expenses just get reported on Schedule C of our personal tax return. We're personally liable for any business debts or legal issues, and our business isn't a separate legal entity from us as individuals, but it's simple and free and works fine for many freelancers.

LLC formation creates a separate legal entity that provides liability protection, meaning if our business gets sued or goes into debt, our personal assets like our house and personal savings are generally protected. The protection isn't absolute and can be pierced if we mix business and personal finances too much, which is another reason to keep them completely separate, but it's substantial protection for relatively low cost and complexity.

Setting up an LLC requires filing articles of organization with our state, paying filing fees that range from fifty to five hundred depending on state, and maintaining the LLC properly by keeping separate finances and following state requirements for annual reports or fees. The tax treatment for a single-member LLC is the same as sole proprietorship by default, still using Schedule C, but we can elect to be taxed as an S-corporation if that makes sense for our situation.

S-corporation election makes sense when we're making enough profit that the self-employment tax savings exceed the extra accounting costs and complexity, typically kicking in somewhere around sixty to eighty thousand in profit though the exact number depends on individual circumstances. The benefit comes from splitting our income into salary subject to payroll taxes and distributions not subject to self-employment tax, saving on the Social Security and Medicare taxes we'd otherwise pay on all our profit.

The complexity of S-corp includes running actual payroll for our own salary, filing quarterly payroll tax returns, maintaining proper corporate formalities, and generally needing an accountant to handle everything correctly, which costs money and time. For a freelancer making forty thousand profit annually, the tax savings probably don't exceed the accounting costs, but for one making one hundred thousand profit the savings can be several thousand dollars making it worth the hassle.

Deciding when to upgrade from sole proprietor to LLC or from LLC to S-corp shouldn't happen just because we've heard it's better, but because we've done the math on our specific situation or talked to an accountant who's done the math and shown that the benefits exceed the costs. The freelancer making thirty thousand annually doesn't need an S-corp and might not need an LLC either, while the one making one hundred twenty thousand should probably have both.

The separation between business and personal finances works regardless of business structure, providing clarity and better tax preparation whether we're a sole proprietor with a simple Schedule C or an S-corp with complex accounting requirements. Starting with good financial separation habits as a sole proprietor makes the eventual transition to LLC or S-corp easier because we're already operating like a real business rather than having to suddenly change our whole approach.

Tracking transactions gets infinitely easier when business and personal are separate, because we can connect our business account to our accounting software and have every business transaction automatically categorized without wading through personal spending, and our personal budgeting only needs to track what happens in our personal account without getting confused by business income and expenses. The designer using QuickBooks for business and a simple spreadsheet for personal finances has a clear view of both, while the designer mixing everything in one account and trying to use one tool for tracking has a confused mess.

The psychological benefit of separation is underrated compared to the practical benefits, because seeing our business account balance grow from collecting payments throughout the month then dropping when we pay ourselves salary creates a visible rhythm to our finances that helps us understand how our business is performing. We can see at a glance that business is doing well when the account grows steadily, or needs attention when it's stagnant or declining, information that's invisible when everything's mixed together.

Some freelancers resist the separation because they don't want to deal with managing two accounts, but managing two simple separate accounts is actually easier than managing one complicated mixed account, like how keeping work files and personal files in separate folders is easier than throwing everything into one giant folder and hoping we can find things later. The upfront effort of opening a second account and setting up the transfer system pays off in reduced ongoing complexity every single month going forward.

Starting the separation this week even if our finances are currently a disaster means future months will be cleaner, and we can draw a line saying everything before this date was mixed but everything after is properly separated, giving our accountant a clear cutoff point when tax time comes. We don't need to go back and fix historical mixing, we just need to start doing it right going forward, and the sooner we start the sooner we get the benefits.

Make it Run Themselves

Accounting software feels like unnecessary expense when we're already tight on money and spreadsheets are free, but the hours we waste each month manually tracking transactions and trying to remember what that charge from three weeks ago was for quickly exceed the cost of software that does most of the work automatically. The freelancer spending four hours monthly wrestling with spreadsheets to track income and expenses is wasting time worth at least three to four hundred dollars at typical freelance rates, while paying twenty-five dollars monthly for software that handles the same work in thirty minutes represents a massive return on investment.

The resistance to accounting software usually comes from thinking it's complicated or will require learning a whole new system, when actually most modern options are designed to be simpler than managing spreadsheets manually, automatically importing our bank transactions and categorizing them based on patterns we teach it. The learning curve is real but short, maybe two or three hours to get comfortable with the basics, after which the software saves us time every single month for as long as we use it.

Wave Accounting offers completely free software including income and expense tracking, invoicing, receipt scanning, and basic reporting, making it hard to beat for freelancers just starting to get organized who don't want to spend money on tools. The limitation is that some features like bank connections have limits and support is minimal, but for straightforward freelance finances it works perfectly fine and we can always upgrade to paid software later if we outgrow what Wave offers.

QuickBooks Self-Employed targets freelancers specifically with features designed for our needs like mileage tracking using our phone's GPS, automatic categorization of expenses, quarterly tax estimates based on our income and expenses, and integration with TurboTax for seamless tax filing. The cost runs about fifteen to twenty-five dollars monthly depending on which tier we choose, which is worth it for freelancers making decent income who want more hand-holding and better features than free options provide.

FreshBooks focuses on invoicing and client management while also handling expense tracking and basic accounting, working well for freelancers who send lots of invoices and need professional-looking billing but don't need complex accounting features. The pricing starts around fifteen dollars monthly and scales up based on how many clients we have and which features we need, making it reasonable for established freelancers who are past the barely-getting-by stage.

Choosing which software to use matters way less than actually choosing something and using it consistently, because even basic tracking in simple software beats the elaborate spreadsheet system we set up once and then abandoned after two months. The perfect accounting setup we never actually use is worthless, while the simple tool we check weekly is invaluable, so we should pick based on what we'll actually stick with rather than which has the most impressive feature list.

Setting up whichever software we choose starts with connecting our bank accounts so transactions import automatically instead of requiring manual entry, which is the feature that makes modern accounting software worth using compared to spreadsheets. We provide our bank login credentials or use the bank's API connection depending on which method the software supports, verify that transactions are importing correctly, and then we're done with the hardest part.

Categorizing transactions teaches the software how to handle our specific patterns, starting with the categories we set up based on common expense types like software subscriptions, office supplies, meals, travel, equipment, professional development, and whatever else we regularly spend on. The first month requires actively categorizing each transaction since the software doesn't know our patterns yet, but after that it starts auto-categorizing based on what we taught it, only requiring our attention for unusual transactions.

Rules and automation take categorization further by setting up patterns like all charges from Adobe get categorized as software, all charges from gas stations get categorized as auto expense, all charges from our coworking space get categorized as office expense, eliminating the need to manually categorize recurring charges. Each rule we create saves us a few seconds per transaction, which compounds to meaningful time savings over hundreds of transactions per year.

The monthly review process becomes the foundation of our financial awareness, blocking out two to four hours on our calendar every month to sit down with our accounting software and actually look at what happened financially instead of just hoping things are working out. This isn't optional nice-to-have time, it's critical business-management time that prevents small problems from becoming big crises, and it needs to be protected like any other important appointment.

What we're reviewing during those hours includes total income for the month compared to our planning income and to the same month last year, showing whether we're on track or falling behind. We're looking at total expenses by category compared to what we budgeted and what we spent last month, catching any categories that are creeping upward or any unusual charges that might be errors or fraud. We're checking that our tax savings account is growing appropriately, that our buffer and emergency funds are on track, and that we actually transferred our salary to our personal account.

Questions we're asking ourselves during review include whether income is trending up or down over the past few months, whether any expense categories are consistently over budget and need either increased budget allocation or spending cuts, whether we have any outstanding invoices that need follow-up, and whether any upcoming expenses need planning. The freelancer who skips these reviews and just hopes everything's fine is the one who gets surprised by tax bills they should have seen coming or client relationships souring because they never followed up on late payments.

Real example of monthly review shows a freelancer opening QuickBooks on the first Sunday of the month, seeing they earned sixty-four hundred in September compared to their planning income of fifty-five hundred and sixty-one hundred in September last year, meaning they're ahead of both benchmarks. Expenses totaled twenty-eight hundred including twelve hundred in baseline personal salary, eight hundred in business expenses, and eight hundred going to tax savings, leaving them with positive cash flow of thirty-six hundred for the month.

Drilling into expense categories shows software subscriptions at one hundred eighty compared to budgeted one hundred fifty, office supplies at forty compared to budgeted fifty, meals at ninety compared to budgeted seventy-five, and professional development at two hundred for an online course they took. The software overage is from adding a new tool they're testing, probably fine but worth noting to see if they actually use it enough to justify keeping. The meals overage is from a couple client meetings, also fine but they'll watch it next month to make sure it doesn't become a pattern.

Checking accounts receivable shows three outstanding invoices totaling forty-eight hundred, two of which are within normal payment terms and one that's now fifteen days late, meaning they need to send a polite follow-up email this week. Their tax savings account grew to eighty-six hundred after adding this month's contribution, right on track for their estimated quarterly payment of four thousand due in two weeks. Buffer account is at ninety-two hundred, just over two months of salary saved, and emergency fund is at thirteen thousand, about four months of baseline expenses.

The whole review took ninety minutes including some time to clean up a few miscategorized transactions and update their budget for next month based on what they learned, and now they have complete clarity on their financial situation instead of vague anxiety about whether things are working. They know they need to follow up on one late payment, they know their tax savings is adequate for the upcoming quarterly payment, they know they're building buffer and emergency fund on schedule, and they can make confident decisions about discretionary spending knowing exactly where they stand.

Invoicing systems integrated with accounting software eliminate the friction of creating and sending invoices, which matters because the faster we invoice the faster we get paid, and anything that makes invoicing easier means we'll do it promptly instead of letting it slide. FreshBooks and Wave both include invoicing features, or we can use standalone invoicing tools like Invoicely or Bonsai that connect to our accounting software to keep everything in sync.

Professional invoice templates make us look established and competent rather than like someone winging it with a Word doc, including our business name and logo, clear itemization of what we're billing for, payment terms stating when payment is due, payment methods the client can use, and our contact information for questions. The designer sending a polished invoice with their branding and clear terms gets taken more seriously than the one sending a quickly typed email asking for money.

Payment terms need to be stated explicitly on every invoice rather than assuming clients know when to pay, with common options being net 15, net 30, or due upon receipt depending on our relationship with the client and industry norms. Net 30 means payment is due thirty days from invoice date, which is standard in many industries but also means we're waiting a full month after completing work to get paid, while due upon receipt or net 15 gets us paid faster if clients will accept those terms.

Accepting credit cards and ACH payments through our invoicing system makes it easier for clients to pay quickly rather than having to mail checks or set up bank transfers manually, though we pay processing fees of around three percent for credit cards or one percent for ACH. The cost is worth it if it speeds up payment and reduces our collection effort, and we can always build the fees into our pricing if we don't want to absorb them ourselves.

Late payment follow-up becomes systematic rather than awkward when we have a process, starting with a friendly reminder a few days after the due date saying we're just checking they received the invoice and asking if they have any questions. Most late payments are just client disorganization rather than inability or refusal to pay, and a polite nudge is all it takes to get moved to the top of their payment queue.

The second follow-up a week later if payment still hasn't arrived gets slightly firmer while staying professional, noting that payment is now X days overdue and asking them to confirm when we can expect payment. The third follow-up after another week states clearly that work will pause until the outstanding invoice is paid and future work may require deposits or different payment terms, setting a boundary without being hostile.

Automation features in accounting software include recurring invoices for retainer clients who get billed the same amount monthly, automatic expense categorization based on rules we've set up, scheduled reports that get emailed to us weekly or monthly showing our financial status, and bank feed imports that happen daily without us thinking about it. Each automation removes a small bit of friction and mental load, adding up to significantly less time spent on financial management over the course of a year.

The filing system for receipts and documents can be entirely digital using tools built into our accounting software or separate apps like Shoeboxed or Expensify, photographing paper receipts and uploading them to categorize and store for tax purposes. The IRS accepts digital receipts as valid documentation, making it unnecessary to keep boxes of paper receipts unless we prefer physical backups.

Monthly organization habits keep things from getting overwhelming at year end, like spending fifteen minutes each week uploading receipts for that week's purchases and making sure transactions are categorized correctly, rather than trying to reconstruct everything in March when we're preparing taxes. The freelancer who uploads receipts and categorizes transactions as they happen spends maybe an hour monthly on this task throughout the year, while the one who ignores it until tax season spends eight or ten miserable hours trying to remember what various charges were for.

Annual tax preparation becomes straightforward when we've been maintaining our accounting software all year, because we can just pull reports showing our total income and expenses by category, print or export receipts for anything the accountant needs to see, and have everything ready in an hour or two rather than spending days assembling information from bank statements and memory. Most accounting software has reports specifically designed for tax prep, showing exactly what our accountant needs in the format they need it.

The accountant we work with should be familiar with freelancer taxes and self-employment issues rather than someone who primarily does employee returns, because the deductions and strategies that matter for us are different from what matters for W-2 workers. Finding a good accountant usually means asking other freelancers for recommendations, looking for someone who specializes in small businesses or self-employed clients, and being willing to pay a few hundred dollars for their expertise rather than trying to do everything ourselves with TurboTax.

When to hire an accountant depends on our income level and comfort with tax complexity, but most freelancers earning over fifty thousand annually benefit from professional help, and those earning over a hundred thousand definitely need it because the potential tax savings and mistake avoidance justify the cost multiple times over. The freelancer doing their own taxes with DIY software might miss deductions worth more than the accountant's fee, or make mistakes that trigger penalties exceeding what professional preparation would have cost.

The cost of accounting help runs from three hundred to a thousand or more for annual tax preparation depending on complexity and location, with monthly bookkeeping adding another hundred to three hundred monthly if we want someone handling our accounting throughout the year rather than just at tax time. For most solo freelancers, annual tax prep is sufficient and we can handle monthly bookkeeping ourselves with software, but those with complex situations or very high income might benefit from ongoing professional help.

Time tracking for billable work needs to happen somehow if we're charging hourly or billing projects where we want to know our effective hourly rate, using either built-in features in our accounting software or standalone tools like Toggl or Harvest that integrate with our other systems. The key is making tracking low-friction enough that we actually do it, which usually means using a tool with a simple start and stop button rather than something requiring detailed time entry.

Tracking non-billable time separately from billable time shows us where our working hours actually go and why we can't bill forty hours per week even though we're working full time, revealing the admin tasks and marketing and learning that eat up hours without generating client invoices. This information helps when we're calculating what we need to charge to hit income targets, because we can see that our twenty billable hours per week really represent forty total working hours.

The system we build in this chapter isn't meant to be perfect or permanent, it's meant to be functional and actually used, giving us visibility into our finances without consuming our lives with administrative work. We can always upgrade to better tools or add complexity later if we need it, but starting with something simple that works beats waiting until we have time to build the perfect system that we never actually start using.

Checking that the system is working means looking at whether we're actually using it monthly, whether we're catching financial issues before they become crises, whether tax time is easier than it used to be, and whether we feel more in control of our money than we did before. If the answer to those questions is yes, the system is working regardless of whether it's the most sophisticated setup possible, and if the answer is no we need to simplify or change something because a system we don't use might as well not exist.

Expensive Mistakes

The tax bill that arrives demanding twelve thousand dollars we don't have ruins more freelance businesses than almost any other single mistake, turning a profitable year into a financial crisis because we spent everything that came in without setting aside the thirty percent that was never really ours to spend. The freelancer who earns seventy thousand and spends sixty-eight thinking they're being responsible discovers they owe twenty-two thousand in taxes between self-employment and income tax, creating a fourteen thousand shortfall that takes years to recover from while trying to also save for current year taxes.

Fixing this mistake means starting the automatic thirty percent transfer to tax savings immediately with the very next payment we receive, no exceptions and no waiting until we feel like we can afford it, because we can't afford not to do it. The tax obligation exists whether we save for it or not, and ignoring it just means the IRS will eventually take the money plus penalties and interest, while saving for it means we're in control and ready when quarterly payments come due.

Mixing business and personal finances creates a cascade of problems starting with lost tax deductions because we can't prove which expenses were actually business-related, continuing through inability to see whether our business is profitable or just generating activity, and ending with potential IRS scrutiny if our messy records look like we're not running a legitimate business. The cost shows up as higher taxes from missed deductions, wasted hours at tax time trying to reconstruct everything, and accountant fees for dealing with our disaster.

The solution requires opening a business bank account this week and running all future business transactions through it exclusively, drawing a line at today's date where everything before was mixed but everything after is clean. We don't need to go back and fix historical mixing unless we're getting audited, we just need to stop making the mistake going forward, and six months of clean separation is infinitely better than continuing to mix everything.

Building no emergency fund means living one client loss or one illness away from financial catastrophe, making us desperate enough to take bad clients at low rates because we can't afford to be selective, creating a doom loop where we're always working with difficult clients who don't pay well because we never have the security to turn them down. The real cost isn't just the stress of constant financial precarity, it's the opportunity cost of all the better work we can't pursue because we're stuck grinding for clients who treat us poorly.

Starting emergency fund building means deciding today that ten or fifteen percent of every payment goes to emergency savings before we spend anything else, even if that ten percent is only fifty or a hundred dollars this month. The account balance will grow slowly at first but the habit of saving is what matters, and twelve months of small deposits adds up to several thousand dollars of buffer between us and crisis.

Chronic underpricing keeps us trapped working maximum hours for minimum income, wearing ourselves down physically and mentally while watching less skilled freelancers who charge appropriately earn more for less work. The cost is measured in burnout, in the clients we attract who only care about cheap rates rather than quality work, in the years we spend building a business that can't sustain us instead of one that actually provides the life we wanted when we went freelance.

Raising rates requires accepting that some clients will leave and deciding that's fine because we're trading quantity of low-paying clients for quality of appropriately-paying clients, which means less total work and more total income. We set our new rate at what the work is actually worth, we inform current clients with appropriate notice, we quote new prospects at the new rate immediately, and we trust that clients who value our work will pay what we're worth.

Not tracking expenses means leaving thousands of dollars in tax deductions on the table every year, essentially overpaying our taxes because we can't prove we had legitimate business expenses that would reduce our taxable income. The freelancer spending five thousand annually on software, equipment, professional development, and other deductible expenses but not tracking them pays fifteen hundred more in taxes than necessary at a thirty percent tax rate, money that could have gone toward emergency fund or retirement instead.

The fix is simple enough that there's no excuse for not doing it, either using accounting software that imports and categorizes transactions automatically or at minimum saving all receipts and noting what they were for in a spreadsheet. Spending two hours monthly on expense tracking saves us hundreds or thousands at tax time, making it some of the highest-paid work we do even though it feels like tedious admin.

Budgeting based on our best month sets us up for constant disappointment and financial stress when normal months feel like failure because they don't match the peak we're comparing against, while also encouraging spending at a level we can't sustain. The freelancer who earned ten thousand in March and builds their budget around that income struggles every other month when they earn six thousand, feeling broke despite earning above their actual baseline.

Using our lowest recent month or a conservative average as our planning income means most months feel like wins because we exceed our baseline, extra money goes toward buffer and savings making us more secure, and we're never scrambling to cover basic expenses during slow periods. The psychological shift from feeling constantly behind to feeling generally ahead makes the conservative planning worth it even if we're leaving money unspent in good months.

Ignoring retirement means we're building a business that supports us today but leaves us with nothing when we can't work anymore, forcing us to keep freelancing into our sixties or seventies not because we enjoy it but because we have no savings to retire on. The cost of starting retirement saving at forty instead of thirty is hundreds of thousands in lost compound growth, and the cost of never starting at all is working until we physically can't anymore.

Opening a SEP IRA or Solo 401k takes maybe an hour through providers like Vanguard or Fidelity, and contributing even five or ten percent of our income makes a massive difference over decades. The freelancer who starts saving three hundred monthly at thirty has over four hundred thousand by sixty-five assuming seven percent growth, while the one who waits until forty ends up with under two hundred thousand saving the same monthly amount.

Forgetting to account for non-billable time when calculating our hourly rate means we think we're earning ninety dollars per hour because that's what we charge, but we're really earning forty-five per hour because half our working time goes to unbillable admin, marketing, and overhead. This misunderstanding leads to pricing ourselves too low and wondering why we can't make ends meet despite charging what seems like good rates.

Tracking our actual time for a few weeks shows the real split between billable and non-billable hours, usually revealing we're billing maybe twenty to twenty-five hours weekly even when working forty or more, and this information tells us we need to either charge way more per hour or transition to project pricing that isn't tied to time spent. The developer who discovers they're only billing twenty hours weekly instead of the thirty they assumed needs to raise their hourly rate by fifty percent just to earn what they thought they were already making.

Skipping health insurance because the premiums seem expensive compared to our current income creates catastrophic risk where one serious illness or accident could cost tens or hundreds of thousands, bankrupting us and destroying everything we've built. The monthly premium might be three or four hundred which feels like a lot, but it's nothing compared to the fifty thousand hospital bill for a three-day stay or the ongoing costs of managing a chronic condition without coverage.

Getting covered through the health insurance marketplace, a spouse's plan, or professional association options needs to happen even if it means cutting other expenses or working harder to increase income, because this is non-negotiable protection. The freelancer who skips insurance to save money and then gets diagnosed with something requiring ongoing treatment faces a choice between bankruptcy and going without care, neither of which is acceptable.

Allowing scope creep where we keep doing "just one more thing" for clients without adjusting our price trains them to expect free work and leaves us working way more hours than we're being paid for, creating resentment that eventually damages or ends the relationship anyway. The designer who agreed to create a logo for twelve hundred but ends up also designing business cards and a website header and social media templates has done three thousand dollars of work for twelve hundred, effectively cutting their rate to less than half.

Setting clear boundaries in our contracts about what's included and what constitutes additional work requiring separate payment protects us from our own tendency to be helpful beyond what's reasonable, and learning to politely decline or requote when clients ask for extras keeps the relationship professional. The response to "can you just quickly do this other thing" is "absolutely, let me send you a quote for that addition" rather than "sure, no problem" followed by internal resentment about free work.

Real story of tax disaster shows a freelancer earning eighty-five thousand over the year, spending everything as it came in on living expenses and business costs and treating themselves occasionally to nice things because they were doing well, then discovering at tax time they owed twenty-eight thousand in combined federal, state, and self-employment taxes. They had maybe three thousand in savings, creating a twenty-five thousand shortfall that required setting up a payment plan with the IRS, paying penalties and interest, and spending the next eighteen months living on bare minimum while catching up.

That disaster was completely preventable by setting aside thirty percent of each payment throughout the year, which would have created twenty-five thousand in tax savings ready to pay the bill, but the freelancer thought they'd figure it out later and later turned into crisis. The recovery took nearly two years of extreme financial stress, during which they also had to save for current year taxes while paying off last year's debt, leaving almost nothing for actually living.

Another real story shows a freelancer losing their major client who represented sixty percent of their income, going from earning eight thousand monthly to earning three thousand, with no emergency fund to cushion the drop. They immediately fell behind on rent, maxed out credit cards trying to cover the gap, took any work they could find at terrible rates just to get some income, and spent six months climbing out of debt while rebuilding their client base.

The same situation with a six-month emergency fund would have played out completely differently, giving them breathing room to selectively pursue good clients instead of desperately taking anything, maintaining their rates instead of slashing them, and ending up in a stronger position after replacing the lost client with several better ones. The cost of not having emergency fund was months of stress, thousands in credit card interest, and damaged professional reputation from taking low-quality work.

A third story involves a freelancer who underpiced their services for three years, charging forty dollars per hour when the market rate was ninety, working fifty-hour weeks to earn fifty thousand annually when they should have been earning ninety thousand or more working fewer hours. The cost was three years of unnecessary struggle, complete burnout that nearly drove them to quit freelancing entirely, and a client base full of bargain hunters who complained about everything despite getting incredible value.

They finally raised rates to eighty dollars per hour, lost about half their clients immediately, but the remaining clients plus a few new ones at the higher rate meant they earned sixty-five thousand working thirty hours weekly instead of fifty thousand at fifty hours. Within a year they were earning ninety thousand at thirty-five hours weekly, had rebuilt their client base with people who respected their expertise, and actually enjoyed their work again instead of resenting every project.

The pattern across all these mistakes is that short-term thinking creates long-term problems that cost way more to fix than they would have cost to prevent, whether it's spending tax money we should have saved, skipping emergency fund contributions, underpricing our work, or allowing scope creep. The pain of saving thirty percent for taxes is real but temporary, while the pain of owing the IRS twenty-five thousand we don't have lasts for years.

Warning signs that we're heading toward these mistakes include checking our bank balance multiple times daily hoping it magically increased, avoiding looking at our accounting software because we're worried what we'll find, feeling constant low-level anxiety about money despite earning decent income, taking every client who contacts us regardless of rate or fit because we feel like we can't afford to turn anyone down, and making financial decisions based on what we hope will happen rather than what's actually happening.

Catching these patterns early means we can course-correct before they become full-blown crises, like noticing we've skipped tax savings for two months and immediately resuming instead of waiting until we've skipped six months and the problem is much bigger. The monthly financial review we set up in the previous chapter exists specifically to catch these issues while they're still small, giving us the information we need to adjust before small problems compound into disasters.

Course corrections that work include immediately restarting automatic transfers for whatever we've been skipping even if the amount is smaller than it should be because something is infinitely better than nothing, raising our rates for all new work starting today even if we're scared clients won't pay it, opening the emergency fund savings account we've been putting off and making the first deposit however small, and having the difficult conversation with existing clients about scope boundaries before resentment destroys the relationship.

Getting professional help makes sense when we've made one of these mistakes and don't know how to fix it ourselves, whether that's hiring an accountant to help negotiate with the IRS about tax debt, working with a financial planner to build a real emergency fund and retirement plan, or bringing in a business coach to help us raise rates and position ourselves properly. The cost of professional help is almost always less than the cost of continuing to struggle alone, and the expertise they bring can compress months or years of trial and error into a few focused sessions.

When to get help depends on the size of the problem and our ability to fix it ourselves, but generally if we've made the same mistake multiple times despite knowing better, or if the financial stakes are high enough that getting it wrong could seriously damage our business, professional guidance is worth the investment. The freelancer who owes fifteen thousand to the IRS should absolutely hire a tax professional rather than trying to handle it alone, and the one who's been underpricing for years might benefit from a coach who can help them raise rates strategically.

The underlying theme connecting all these mistakes is not having systems in place to prevent them, which is why the previous chapters focused so heavily on building automatic transfers, separate accounts, regular reviews, and clear processes. When we have systems running, most of these mistakes become impossible or at least much harder to make, because the system catches us before we've gone too far wrong.

Recovering from mistakes we've already made starts with stopping the behavior that caused the problem, even if we can't immediately fix all the damage. The freelancer in tax debt needs to start saving thirty percent immediately even though they're also paying off past debt, because otherwise they're just creating next year's crisis while dealing with last year's. The one who's been underpricing needs to raise rates for new clients today even though existing clients are still at old rates, because at least new relationships start on proper footing.

The recovery timeline depends on the severity of the mistake but usually runs six to eighteen months for major issues like significant tax debt or completely depleted savings, requiring sustained discipline and probably some sacrifice of lifestyle to get back on track. The freelancer rebuilding from zero emergency fund to six months saved while also maintaining tax savings and buffer might need a year or more of saving twenty or thirty percent of income, which means living on less than they could otherwise afford.

Accepting that recovery takes time without getting discouraged and giving up is crucial, because the alternative to slowly fixing the problem is leaving it unfixed, which just makes it worse. The freelancer who owes the IRS fifteen thousand and commits to paying it off while also building proper financial habits going forward will be in much better shape in two years than the one who gives up and lets the debt grow while continuing to make the same mistakes.

Prevention is obviously better than recovery for all of these mistakes, which is why getting the systems right from the start matters so much, but for those of us who've already made some of these mistakes the good news is that they're fixable with enough discipline and time. We don't have to be perfect, we just have to be willing to acknowledge what's not working and change it.

Building Long-Term Wealth

Retirement planning as a freelancer means accepting that nobody's going to build this for us the way employers build it for their workers through 401k matches and pension contributions, so we either take responsibility for saving and investing now or we work until our bodies give out because we have no other option. The employee who contributes five percent to their 401k and gets a five percent match is effectively saving ten percent with half of it being free money, while we're saving zero percent unless we actively choose to open accounts and make contributions ourselves.

The psychological barrier is that retirement feels impossibly far away when we're struggling to manage this month's cash flow, making it easy to justify putting off retirement savings until we're more stable financially, but waiting costs us the most valuable resource we have for building wealth which is time for compound growth to work. The thirty-year-old who starts saving three hundred monthly ends up with way more at sixty-five than the forty-year-old who saves six hundred monthly, even though the forty-year-old contributes more total dollars, because those extra ten years of compound growth matter more than the contribution amount.

Traditional IRA contributions reduce our taxable income in the year we make them, potentially saving us thirty percent or more in taxes depending on our bracket, making a six thousand contribution really only cost us four thousand after accounting for the tax savings. The money grows tax-deferred until we withdraw it in retirement, at which point we pay ordinary income tax on distributions, but the decades of tax-free growth usually make this worthwhile compared to paying taxes upfront and investing in a taxable account.

The contribution limit for traditional IRA sits at seven thousand for 2025, or eight thousand if we're fifty or older and eligible for catch-up contributions, which isn't a huge amount but it's enough to start building retirement savings if we're consistent about maxing it out annually. The freelancer who contributes the full seven thousand every year for thirty years at seven percent average returns ends up with over seven hundred thousand by retirement, which generates around thirty thousand annually in safe withdrawal rates.

Roth IRA contributions don't reduce our current taxes but grow completely tax-free and come out tax-free in retirement, making them attractive when we expect to be in a higher tax bracket later or just want the certainty of knowing we'll never owe taxes on that money again. The contribution limits match traditional IRA at seven thousand annually, but Roth has income limits that phase out the ability to contribute directly if we make too much, though backdoor Roth conversions can work around this for high earners.

Choosing between traditional and Roth depends on our current tax bracket and our expectations about future taxes, with the general rule being traditional makes more sense when we're in high tax brackets now and expect to be in lower brackets in retirement, while Roth makes more sense when we're in lower brackets now or expect tax rates to rise. For most freelancers earning fifty to one hundred thousand, a mix of both provides tax diversification and flexibility in retirement.

SEP IRA designed specifically for self-employed people allows much higher contributions than traditional or Roth IRAs, letting us contribute up to twenty-five percent of our net self-employment income with a cap around sixty-six thousand for 2024 and likely higher for 2025. This makes SEP IRAs perfect for established freelancers who want to save aggressively for retirement and have the income to support large contributions.

The calculation for SEP contribution limits gets complicated because we're contributing as both employer and employee, but the practical limit works out to about twenty percent of our gross self-employment income after accounting for the self-employment tax deduction. A freelancer earning ninety thousand in profit can contribute around eighteen thousand to a SEP IRA, far more than the seven thousand allowed in traditional or Roth IRAs, making it possible to catch up quickly if we started saving late.

Setting up a SEP IRA takes maybe thirty minutes through providers like Vanguard, Fidelity, or Schwab, filling out forms that ask basic information about our business and choosing what to invest in, with low-cost index funds being the standard recommendation for most people who don't want to actively manage investments. The contributions are tax-deductible just like traditional IRA, reducing our current tax bill while building retirement savings.

Solo 401k provides even more flexibility than SEP IRA for freelancers with no employees, allowing contributions as both employer and employee that can total over sixty-six thousand annually for those earning enough to max it out. The employee contribution portion goes up to twenty-three thousand, or thirty thousand five hundred if we're fifty or older, and then we can add employer contributions on top of that up to the overall limit.

The advantage of Solo 401k over SEP IRA is the higher total contribution limits and the ability to make Roth contributions if we choose that option, while the disadvantage is more administrative complexity requiring annual filings once the account balance exceeds two hundred fifty thousand. For freelancers earning over one hundred thousand who want to save aggressively, Solo 401k usually beats SEP IRA, but for those earning less or wanting simplicity, SEP IRA is fine.

Starting retirement contributions small and increasing them over time works better than waiting until we can afford some ideal amount, because saving two hundred monthly starting now beats saving six hundred monthly starting in five years due to the power of early compound growth. The investment account that starts with small contributions today and grows as our income grows will end up larger than the one we waited to start until we were making more money.

Real example shows a freelancer earning sixty thousand annually who decides to contribute five percent or three thousand to a SEP IRA, which reduces their taxable income and saves them about nine hundred in taxes, making the real cost of the contribution twenty-one hundred. After three years of consistent contributions they've saved nine thousand plus growth, and their income has increased to seventy-five thousand so they raise their contribution percentage to eight percent or six thousand annually.

Investment strategy for variable income can't rely on fixed monthly contributions the way employee retirement savings does, because some months we're flush and others we're tight, making it better to contribute quarterly or annually based on our actual income than to commit to monthly amounts we might not be able to maintain. Setting aside a percentage of profit specifically for retirement and letting it accumulate in savings until we make our quarterly or annual contribution gives us flexibility while still making consistent progress.

The percentage-based approach to retirement investing means we decide something like ten percent of our net profit goes to retirement regardless of whether that's two hundred this month or a thousand, automatically scaling with our income so we're never struggling to make a fixed contribution during slow months. The freelancer earning variable monthly income between four and eight thousand might contribute anywhere from four hundred to eight hundred monthly, averaging around six hundred if their average income is six thousand.

The threshold method works by setting an income level above which we start investing aggressively, like deciding that any month we earn over six thousand we invest fifty percent of everything above that threshold. This ensures we're covering baseline needs first before trying to invest, while still building wealth during good months. The freelancer who earns eight thousand in a good month would invest one thousand under this approach, while a month they only earn five thousand means zero investment but also no stress about forcing contributions they can't afford.

Windfall strategy takes large one-time payments from projects and immediately allocates a significant portion to retirement before the money gets absorbed into general spending, making it easy to boost retirement savings substantially a few times per year. The consultant who receives a twenty thousand payment for a big project might immediately move five to eight thousand into retirement accounts, taking advantage of the large payment to make significant progress without affecting their regular monthly budget.

Where to invest retirement money matters less than most people think because the difference between low-cost index funds at different providers is minimal, but it matters more than nothing because high-fee actively managed funds can cost us hundreds of thousands in lost returns over decades. Vanguard, Fidelity, and Schwab all offer excellent low-cost index fund options, with total market funds or target-date funds being simple default choices that work well for most freelancers who don't want to actively manage investments.

Target-date funds automatically adjust their asset allocation to become more conservative as we approach retirement, starting aggressive with mostly stocks when we're young and gradually shifting toward bonds as we get older. The freelancer who's thirty-five and planning to retire at sixty-five would choose a 2055 target-date fund that handles all the allocation decisions for them, making investing as simple as choosing one fund and contributing to it regularly.

Total stock market index funds provide broader diversification across thousands of companies with extremely low fees, typically around point zero four percent annually, giving us exposure to the entire market's growth without requiring us to pick individual stocks or pay high management fees. Combining a total stock market fund with a total bond market fund in whatever allocation matches our risk tolerance creates a simple two-fund portfolio that covers all our investment needs.

Diversifying income streams beyond just client work creates multiple sources of money coming in, reducing the risk that losing one client or having one slow month tanks our entire income. The writer who earns money from client work, a self-published book, an online course, and affiliate commissions from recommending products is more financially stable than the writer who only earns from client work, even if the total annual income is similar.

Passive income sources take time and effort to build initially but can generate money with minimal ongoing work once established, like creating a template or digital product we sell repeatedly, building an email list we monetize through affiliate partnerships, or developing a course we sell without having to deliver it live each time. The designer who creates and sells website templates on a marketplace might earn an extra thousand monthly with minimal ongoing effort after the initial creation work.

Adding related services to our core offering increases income without requiring us to learn completely new skills, like the developer who primarily builds websites adding ongoing maintenance retainers, or the writer who primarily creates content adding editing and strategy consulting. These additions use expertise we already have while diversifying our revenue sources and creating different income patterns that smooth out the overall variability.

Real example of income diversification shows a freelance designer earning forty-eight hundred monthly from client work, adding twelve hundred from selling templates on Creative Market, eight hundred from a group coaching program they run quarterly, and three hundred from affiliate commissions on tools they recommend. Total monthly income averages sixty-seven hundred compared to the forty-eight hundred they'd earn from only client work, and the mix means slow months for client work don't drop total income as dramatically.

Investment accounts for money beyond retirement need to be kept separate from retirement savings because we might need to access this money before age fifty-nine and a half, making it unsuitable for IRA or 401k accounts that charge penalties for early withdrawal. Opening a regular taxable brokerage account at the same provider where we have our retirement accounts simplifies management while giving us access to the same investment options without the withdrawal restrictions.

The taxable account gets funded after we've maxed out tax-advantaged retirement accounts or when we have money we might need within the next decade, investing in similar low-cost index funds but accepting that we'll pay taxes on dividends and capital gains annually instead of deferring them. The benefit is complete flexibility to withdraw whenever we want without penalties, making this where we invest money we're saving for goals like buying a house or funding a sabbatical or just building wealth beyond retirement.

Insurance becomes more important not less as we build wealth because we have more to lose if something goes wrong, with health insurance being absolutely non-negotiable, disability insurance protecting our ability to earn income, and life insurance mattering if anyone depends on our income. The freelancer with fifty thousand in emergency fund and growing retirement accounts needs to protect their ability to keep earning and contributing, which means having insurance against major risks.

Health insurance through the marketplace, a spouse's employer, or professional associations protects against medical costs that could wipe out years of savings in one illness, making it worth paying premiums even when we're young and healthy. The monthly cost might be three to five hundred or more depending on our age and location and income, but this is non-negotiable protection that prevents catastrophic financial loss.

Disability insurance replaces our income if we become unable to work due to illness or injury, paying us a percentage of our normal income for as long as we're disabled up to the policy limits. This matters more for freelancers than employees because we have no company disability coverage, no paid sick leave, and no safety net if we can't work. The cost varies based on our age, health, income, and what percentage we want covered, but typically runs one to three percent of our income for good coverage.

Life insurance only matters if someone depends on our income like a spouse or children who would struggle financially if we died, replacing our earning power so they can maintain their lifestyle or pay off debts we'd otherwise have left them with. Term life insurance provides coverage for a specific period like twenty or thirty years at low cost, usually under a hundred monthly for hundreds of thousands in coverage for healthy people in their thirties or forties.

Professional liability insurance protects against lawsuits claiming our work caused financial damage to a client, covering legal defense costs and potential settlements up to the policy limits. This matters more in some fields than others, with consultants and advisors facing higher risk than designers or writers, but the peace of mind of knowing one angry client can't bankrupt us through a lawsuit is worth considering regardless of field.

The wealth-building timeline for freelancers typically follows a pattern where year one focuses on survival and stability through building emergency fund and establishing tax systems, year two adds retirement contributions and higher income through better pricing, and year three and beyond compounds previous progress while adding diversification and investment growth. This isn't a rigid schedule but a general progression that most successful freelancers follow.

Year one goals include having three to six months of baseline expenses in emergency fund, tax savings running smoothly with no surprises at quarterly payment time, buffer account holding at least two months of salary, and business and personal finances completely separated. These fundamentals create the stability we need to focus on growth rather than constantly managing crisis.

Year two goals build on that foundation by starting retirement contributions even if they're small, raising rates at least once to increase income by twenty to thirty percent, diversifying our client base so no single client represents more than thirty percent of income, and potentially exploring one passive income stream. The focus shifts from survival to actually building wealth.

Year three and beyond accelerates what's working from previous years, with emergency fund growing toward twelve months if it's not there already, retirement contributions increasing as income grows, passive income streams becoming meaningful parts of our total income, and potentially making first serious investments outside retirement accounts. This is where financial stability turns into actual wealth building.

Real progression over three years shows a freelancer starting with zero savings and sixty thousand annual income from client work, adding twelve thousand to emergency fund in year one while establishing tax and buffer systems, contributing seven thousand to retirement in year two while growing income to seventy-five thousand through rate increases, and contributing twelve thousand to retirement plus five thousand to taxable investments in year three while growing income to ninety thousand partly through adding passive income streams.

The compounding effect of these choices means year three doesn't just have the current year's contributions but also the growth on previous years' investments, so the freelancer with thirty-four thousand invested total might see that grow to forty-two thousand with market gains, making it easier to reach the next milestone. Each year the foundation gets stronger and the progress gets faster, assuming we stay disciplined about the systems we've built.

Knowing when we've made it financially as a freelancer comes when we can weather a three-month dry spell without panic, when we're confidently turning down clients who don't meet our rate or quality standards, when retirement accounts are growing steadily, and when we're making financial decisions based on what we want rather than what we desperately need. This might take three years or seven years depending on our starting point and income level, but the trajectory is what matters more than the exact timeline.

The goal isn't perfection or reaching some arbitrary wealth number, it's building a sustainable financial life that lets us do work we enjoy with clients we respect while knowing we're protected against major risks and building toward a retirement where we don't have to keep working. Getting there requires discipline and time, but for those willing to put in both, the freelance life can provide not just freedom and flexibility but genuine long-term financial security.

The 90-Day Plan

Starting everything at once guarantees we'll get overwhelmed and quit within two weeks, while starting with one small action this week and adding more as we build momentum gives us a realistic shot at actually transforming our financial situation over the next three months. The freelancer who tries to open accounts, start tracking, build buffer, save for taxes, and raise rates all in the same week burns out fast, while the one who tackles setup in phases builds sustainable habits that stick.

The first two weeks focus entirely on assessment and gathering information rather than making changes, because we need to know our current reality before we can build systems to improve it. Trying to fix things before we understand what's broken leads to solutions that don't match our actual problems, wasting effort on the wrong priorities while missing what really matters.

Week one starts Monday morning by pulling up our bank statements for the past six months, downloading them as PDFs or printing them if we prefer paper, and blocking out three hours sometime this week to actually read through them line by line. We're looking for every transaction over that six-month period, noting what we spent money on, what we earned from clients, and starting to see patterns in our spending and income that we've been too busy to notice.

While we have those statements open we're adding up total income for each of the six months, writing those numbers down somewhere we won't lose them, calculating the average by adding all six months together and dividing by six. We're also finding the lowest month in that six-month period and writing that number down separately, because that's going to be important for our conservative planning income later.

The expense side gets similar treatment where we're categorizing every charge into groups like rent, utilities, groceries, gas, eating out, subscriptions, business software, business equipment, and whatever other categories make sense for our specific spending. This takes the bulk of our three hours because there are hundreds of transactions to sort through, but by the end we have a clear picture of where money actually goes instead of where we think it goes.

Week two continues the assessment by focusing on expenses we can't see in bank statements, specifically the annual or quarterly charges that don't show up in our six-month window but still need to be accounted for. We're making a list of everything we know we pay once or twice a year like insurance premiums, professional licenses, domain renewals, conference tickets, holiday spending, and software we pay annually instead of monthly.

Taking each of those irregular expenses and dividing by twelve gives us the monthly amount we need to set aside so we're not surprised when the bill comes due, and adding up all those monthly amounts tells us how much invisible expense we have that's not reflected in our regular monthly spending. The freelancer who discovers they have two thousand in annual expenses they'd been ignoring now knows they need to budget an extra one hundred sixty-seven monthly or they'll keep getting blindsided.

By the end of week two we're calculating our baseline essential expenses by adding up only the costs we truly cannot skip like housing, utilities, minimum food budget, insurance, transportation, and minimum debt payments. This number is different from our total spending and probably quite a bit lower, representing what we need to survive rather than what we currently spend when we have the money.

Week three shifts from assessment to setup, opening the accounts and choosing the tools we'll need to run our new financial systems. Monday of week three we're researching business bank accounts and picking one based on the criteria we covered in chapter eight, either going with an online option like Found or Axos for no fees, or a traditional bank if we value branch access enough to deal with their requirements.

The actual account opening happens Tuesday or Wednesday after we've made our choice, filling out the online application with our business information or our personal information if we're a sole proprietor, providing our Social

Security number or EIN, and answering questions about our expected account activity. Most applications get approved within a day or two, and we're getting the account details and debit card in the mail by the end of the week.

While we're waiting for business account approval we're opening a dedicated tax savings account, either at the same bank as our business account for easy transfers or at a high-yield savings bank for better interest rates. This takes maybe fifteen minutes online, and we want it completely separate from our regular savings so there's no temptation to raid tax money for other purposes.

Thursday or Friday of week three we're choosing accounting software based on what we learned in chapter nine, probably starting with Wave if we want free or QuickBooks Self-Employed if we're willing to pay for more features and hand-holding. The setup process includes connecting our bank accounts once they're active, setting up expense categories that match our business, and importing the past few months of transactions to get started.

Week four focuses on the calculations and decisions that will drive our financial systems going forward, using the data we gathered in weeks one and two. We're taking our six-month average income and our lowest month income, deciding which to use as our planning income based on how conservative we want to be, and writing that number down as our baseline for budgeting.

Next we're taking our baseline essential expenses from week two and comparing them to our planning income, seeing how much margin we have between what we need to spend and what we can reliably expect to earn. If planning income is fifty-five hundred and baseline is thirty-eight hundred, we have seventeen hundred of margin to work with for taxes, savings, and variable spending.

From that margin we're calculating our self-salary, probably setting it right at or just above our baseline essential expenses to leave as much margin as possible in the business account for buffer building. Using the example above, we might set salary at forty thousand monthly, leaving the business account to handle the fifteen hundred difference between that and our planning income after we've saved for taxes.

The tax savings calculation is straightforward because we're just committing to thirty percent of every payment regardless of actual tax obligation, simplifying the decision and ensuring we're always oversaving rather than undersaving. We're setting up the automatic transfer if our bank supports it or creating a reminder to manually transfer thirty percent every time a payment hits the business account.

Month two begins the actual implementation where we're living with the systems we set up rather than just planning them, and this is where theory meets reality and we find out what works and what needs adjustment. The first of the month we're making our first official salary transfer from business account to personal account, moving our predetermined salary amount even if the business account balance is lower than we'd like.

Every payment that comes in during month two triggers our thirty percent tax transfer, moving that money immediately to tax savings before we're tempted to spend it on anything else. The first time we do this it feels weird and slightly painful to watch thirty percent disappear, but by the third or fourth payment it becomes routine and we stop thinking about that money as ours to spend.

We're tracking every expense in our accounting software, either through automatic bank feeds that import transactions daily or through manual entry if we prefer more control. Each transaction gets categorized as it comes in, teaching the software our patterns so it can auto-categorize similar transactions in the future, gradually reducing the time this task requires.

The first monthly review happens at the end of month two or beginning of month three, looking at what actually happened compared to what we planned. We're comparing actual income to our planning income seeing whether we hit our target or fell short, actual expenses to our baseline budget seeing where we overspent or underspent, and checking that our tax savings and salary transfers happened as intended.

Month three is about refinement based on what we learned during month two, adjusting our numbers and systems to better match reality instead of assumptions. If we discovered our baseline was too low because we forgot about a regular expense, we're increasing it and adjusting our salary accordingly. If our planning income was too conservative and we've consistently beaten it, we might cautiously increase it while staying below our actual average.

The second salary transfer happens at the beginning of month three, and by now it should feel more routine than it did the first time. The second monthly review at the end of month three gives us comparison data to the first month, showing whether we're making progress on buffer building, whether tax savings is on track, and whether our spending patterns are stabilizing or still fluctuating wildly.

By the end of ninety days we should have business and personal finances completely separated with all transactions flowing through the right accounts, automatic or systematic tax savings happening with every payment, a consistent salary transfer running monthly, some amount of buffer building in the business account even if it's not the full three months yet, and clear visibility into our financial situation through accounting software and monthly reviews.

What we probably don't have yet is a full emergency fund since that takes longer to build, perfect adherence to our budget since we're still learning our real spending patterns, or complete confidence in all our numbers since three months isn't quite enough data. That's fine because ninety days was never about reaching perfection, it was about building systems that will carry us toward stability over the next year and beyond.

The six-month milestone builds on our ninety-day foundation with goals that are achievable but meaningful, starting with having at least one month of baseline expenses in emergency fund even if we're not at the full six months yet. We're checking that our tax savings account has enough to cover our next quarterly payment with some buffer, ideally holding about four to five months worth of the thirty percent we're saving.

Our buffer in the business account should be approaching or exceeding two months of salary by six months in, depending on how much margin we had between planning income and actual income. The freelancer who had a thousand monthly margin should have built five to six thousand in buffer by this point, while the one with only three hundred monthly margin might have fifteen to eighteen hundred, and both are fine because they're moving in the right direction.

We should have completed at least one rate increase for new clients even if we haven't transitioned all existing clients yet, pushing our effective hourly rate or project rates up by ten to twenty percent from where we started. The designer who was charging sixty per hour and is now charging seventy for new work has increased their income potential by seventeen percent, which compounds significantly over a year.

The one-year milestone represents substantial transformation from where we started, with goals that felt impossible at day one but are achievable with consistent effort. Emergency fund should hold at least three months of baseline expenses and ideally closer to six months, providing genuine security against client loss or income disruption instead of just theoretical protection.

Tax savings should have successfully covered all quarterly payments throughout the year with no surprises or scrambling to find money, and we should have a clear sense of our actual tax rate so we can adjust the thirty percent up or down if needed. The freelancer who saved thirty percent but only owed twenty-six can drop to twenty-seven or twenty-eight going forward, freeing up a bit more cash flow for other priorities.

Buffer should be fully built at three months of salary or more, eliminating the stress of month-to-month income variability because we know the buffer will cover us during slow periods. Income should have increased twenty to thirty percent from our starting point through some combination of rate increases, more billable hours, and additional clients at better rates.

We should have made at least some retirement contributions even if they're not huge, opening whichever account type makes sense and funding it with whatever percentage of income we can sustainably contribute. The freelancer making seventy-five thousand who contributes five percent or thirty-seven fifty annually isn't maxing out their retirement options but they're building the habit and making progress.

The two-year milestone takes us from financial stability to actually building wealth, with emergency fund reaching the full six to twelve months of baseline expenses that provides bulletproof protection against almost any crisis. The freelancer with forty-five hundred in monthly baseline expenses and fifty-four thousand in emergency fund can survive a year without income, making them essentially crisis-proof barring catastrophic scenarios.

Retirement contributions should be increasing as income grows, ideally reaching ten to fifteen percent of income or more for those in their thirties and forties who need to make up for starting late. The freelancer earning ninety thousand who contributes ten percent or nine thousand annually is making real progress toward retirement security, and increasing that to fifteen percent as income grows means meaningful wealth building.

Income diversification should be underway with at least one passive or semi-passive income stream beyond direct client work, whether that's a digital product, an online course, affiliate relationships, or some other model that generates money without requiring us to trade hours for dollars. The writer earning fifty-five hundred monthly from client work plus eight hundred from book sales and three hundred from affiliate commissions has thirteen percent of income coming from non-client sources.

Business entity optimization might be worth considering at the two-year mark for those earning over sixty thousand consistently, talking to an accountant about whether LLC or S-corp status would save enough in taxes to justify the additional complexity and cost. The freelancer earning one hundred thousand might save several thousand annually through S-corp election, easily covering the accountant fees and hassle.

The habits we've built over two years of monthly reviews, consistent saving, automatic transfers, and disciplined budgeting become ingrained rather than requiring active willpower, making the systems self-sustaining rather than constantly fighting our natural tendencies. The freelancer who's been paying themselves a salary and saving for taxes for twenty-four months doesn't even think about it anymore, it's just how they operate.

Revisiting and adjusting our systems every six months keeps them aligned with our current reality as our business grows and our situation changes, because the numbers that made sense when we were earning sixty thousand don't necessarily make sense at ninety thousand. We're checking whether our planning income still matches our actual income patterns, whether our baseline expenses have increased with lifestyle inflation, whether our tax savings percentage is still appropriate.

We're also evaluating whether our budget categories still make sense or need to be split differently, whether our accounting software is still serving us well or if we've outgrown it, and whether our rates are still competitive or if we need another increase. The annual rate increase of ten to fifteen percent should be standard practice by this point, keeping our pricing aligned with our growing experience and market rates.

The point where we know the systems are working comes when financial stress drops from constant background anxiety to occasional mild concern during unusually tough periods, when we're making financial decisions confidently instead of guessing and hoping, and when we can weather a slow month without panic because we know our buffer and emergency fund are there. This might happen at six months for some freelancers or take the full two years for others depending on their starting situation.

What success looks like is different for each of us based on our goals and values, but generally includes having enough money saved that we can turn down clients who are terrible to work with, being able to take a week off without financial stress, knowing we'll be fine if a major client leaves, and making progress toward retirement instead of just surviving month to month. The freelancer who can confidently say yes to all those things has built genuine financial security.

The transformation from where most freelancers start to where we can be after implementing these systems is dramatic enough to feel like a completely different life, moving from constant stress about money to confident control over our financial situation, from taking every client regardless of fit to being selective about who we work with, from wondering how we'll retire to watching retirement accounts grow steadily. Getting there requires ninety days of focused effort to build the foundation followed by months and years of maintaining the systems we built, but the payoff in reduced stress and increased security is worth every hour we put in.

Starting Monday with week one's assessment task means by this time next quarter we'll have systems running instead of chaos, clarity instead of confusion, and progress toward stability instead of staying stuck in the invoice-to-invoice cycle. The choice is whether to start now or keep putting it off hoping things will somehow get better on their own, and only one of those choices actually works.

Don't miss out!

Visit the website below and you can sign up to receive emails whenever Ryan Papadopoulos publishes a new book. There's no charge and no obligation.

https://books2read.com/r/B-A-FNUUE-OTJYI

BOOKS 2 READ

Connecting independent readers to independent writers.

Did you love *The Freelancer's Budget: Managing Irregular Income, Planning for Taxes, and Stopping the Invoice-to-Invoice Cycle*? Then you should read *Get Promoted: Visibility Beats Performance Every Time*[1] by Leila Brandt!

[2]

You work late. You deliver results. You volunteer for everything. Meanwhile, the person who leaves at 5 pm every day just got promoted to the role you've been working toward for three years.

Why? In organizations with multiple management layers, promotions don't follow performance. They follow visibility, trust plus timing. Your excellent work is invisible to the people making decisions about your career.

Only twenty-five percent of promotion decisions are based on work quality. The other seventy-five percent? Whether the right people know who you are, whether they trust you can handle more responsibility, and whether budget and timing align.

Here's the other seventy-five percent explained.

---

1. https://books2read.com/u/bMgkX7
2. https://books2read.com/u/bMgkX7

You'll learn why working 60-hour weeks makes you less promotable and what signals you're actually sending. The thank-and-brag method for making work visible without feeling slimy. How to build a promotion case file that makes your manager's advocacy easy. The four questions to ask before taking on any project. Exactly what to say when you formally request a promotion. When company loyalty is costing you years of career progression.

Real talk about the promotion meetings where your future gets decided in thirty seconds. Why executive presence feedback is often code for something else. How to handle being promoted over former peers. The first ninety days after promotion are when most people accidentally derail themselves.

No fluff. No corporate jargon. Just the actual system for getting promoted in large organizations across finance, tech, healthcare, government, and nonprofits.

For mid-level professionals tired of being passed over despite strong performance. People who've been told to keep doing what they're doing for three years while watching others advance. Anyone ready to understand how advancement actually works?

Approximately 35,000 words of specific strategies, conversation scripts, case studies, and frameworks.

Stop playing the game nobody explained.

www.ingramcontent.com/pod-product-compliance
Lightning Source LLC
LaVergne TN
LVHW090420210926
848480LV00002B/633